SpringerBriefs in Computer Science

More information about this series at http://www.springer.com/series/10028

Bin Fan · Zhenhua Wang
Fuchao Wu

Local Image Descriptor: Modern Approaches

 Springer

Bin Fan
Institute of Automation
Chinese Academy of Sciences
Beijing
China

Fuchao Wu
Institute of Automation
Chinese Academy of Sciences
Beijing
China

Zhenhua Wang
School of EEE
Nanyang Technological University
Singapore
Singapore

ISSN 2191-5768   ISSN 2191-5776   (electronic)
SpringerBriefs in Computer Science
ISBN 978-3-662-49171-3   ISBN 978-3-662-49173-7   (eBook)
DOI 10.1007/978-3-662-49173-7

Library of Congress Control Number: 2015959572

Printed on acid-free paper

This Springer imprint is published by SpringerNature
The registered company is Springer-Verlag GmbH Berlin Heidelberg

Foreword 1

Over the last 15 years, feature point descriptors have become indispensable tools in the computer vision community. They are essential components of applications ranging from image retrieval to multi-image stereo matching and from surface reconstruction to image augmentation.

Starting with the original SIFT vector, a great many ways have been proposed to achieve the required invariance to viewpoint and lighting and have achieved high performance levels. The descriptors are usually represented as high-dimensional vectors, such as the 128-dimensional SIFT or the 64-dimensional SURF vectors. While the descriptor's high dimensionality is not an issue when only a few hundreds points need to be represented, it becomes a significant concern when millions have to be on a device with limited computational and storage resources. This happens, for example, when storing all descriptors for a large-scale urban scene on a mobile phone for image-based location purposes. Not only does this require tremendous amounts of storage, it is also slow and potentially unreliable because most recognition algorithms rely on nearest neighbor computations and computing Euclidean distances between long vectors is neither cheap nor optimal.

One traditional way to address these issues is to work with shorter descriptors, which can be achieved by performing dimensionality reduction. However, in recent years, using binary descriptors has emerged as a better alternative. Not only are these descriptors much smaller at very little loss in descriptive power, they can also be compared much faster than floating point ones by using the ability of modern processors to compute the Hamming distance in hardware.

Since there are innumerable ways to compute such binary descriptors ranging from binarizing floating ones to computing them from scratch by using appropriate binary tests, choosing the right one becomes difficult. This is a challenge practitioners must face and this book is designed to help them find their way.

The book moves from traditional floating point, to those that rely on intensity order, and finally to binary ones. It then demonstrates how they can be used in practice and concludes by benchmarking them and making suggestions for future research. Because it covers the whole range from traditional to very recent descriptors and carefully contrasts them, this book is an invaluable guide to a large segment of the computer vision field.

Prof. Pascal Fua
IEEE Fellow
École Polytechnique Fédérale de Lausanne (EPFL)

Foreword 2

Humans receive the great majority of information about their environment through sight. Vision is also the key component for building artificial systems that can perceive and understand their environment. Due to its numerous applications and major research challenges, computer vision is one of the most active research fields in information technology.

In recent years, approaches for effectively describing image contents has been a topic of great interest in the computer vision research. Image descriptors play a key role in most computer vision systems and applications. The function of descriptors is to convert the pixel-level information into a useful form, which captures the most important factors of the imaged scene but is insensitive to irrelevant aspects caused by the varying environment. The effective descriptor is able to ignore the irrelevant aspects caused by the changes in the environment. This should be furthermore done without compromising the descriptive power of the method. While the definition of irrelevant depends on the application, the most common cases are related to imaging conditions like illumination, viewing angle, scale, noise, and blur. Currently, SIFT (scale-invariant feature transform), HOG (histogram of oriented gradients), LBP (local binary pattern), and their variants are the most effective and commonly used descriptors, providing complementary information about the image contents. In many applications, a single descriptor is not enough, but a proper combination of different descriptors should be used.

Image descriptors are normally used in three alternative ways. One is a sparse descriptor, which first detects salient interest points in a given image and then samples a local patch and describes its invariant features. SIFT is the most commonly used sparse descriptor. The second approach is based on computing on a dense grid of uniformly spaced cells. HOG and SIFT are commonly used alternatives for this task. The ordinary texture descriptors are used densely, obtained by regular sampling of the input image or region. In recent years, LBP has been the most widely used dense texture descriptor, but can also be used as a sparse local descriptor like SIFT or computed on a grid like HOG.

My personal research since the early 1990s has contributed to the local binary pattern methodology, its variants, and different applications such as facial image analysis. The great success of the LBP approach shows how important image descriptors are to computer vision and its applications.

This book provides an excellent overview and reference to local image descriptors. After introduction, in Chap. 2 the most common classical local descriptors, including SIFT, SURF, and LBP, are reviewed. Chapter 3 deals with recently proposed intensity order-based descriptors. Chapter 4 introduces binary descriptors, such as BRIEF, ORB, and BRISK, which provide a comparable matching performance with the widely used interest region descriptors (e.g., SIFT and SURF), but have very fast extraction times and very low memory requirements needed, e.g., in emerging applications using mobile devices with limited computational capabilities. Chapter 5 provides instructions for using local descriptors in such modern application problems as structure from motion and 3D reconstruction, object recognition, content-based image retrieval, and simultaneous localization and mapping (SLAM). Chapter 6 introduces commonly used benchmarks for evaluating local image descriptors, and presents conclusions and some future directions for research.

This book provides an excellent overview of local image descriptors and how they can be used for solving various computer vision problems. It also contains references to the most important papers in the field, allowing students to study more details on specific areas. The authors have done an excellent job in writing this book. It will be a valuable resource for researchers, engineers, and graduate students working in computer vision, image analysis, and their applications.

Prof. Matti Pietikäinen
IEEE Fellow, IAPR Fellow
University of Oulu

Preface

Computer vision is an interdiscipline of computer science and artificial intelligence. It aims to make the computer understand and perceive images and videos like human beings, covering lots of typical tasks such as recognition, reconstruction, motion analysis, and so on. Local image descriptor plays a key role in most of these tasks. Especially, since the milestone work of Scale Invariant Feature Transform (SIFT) was systematically proposed in 2004, we have witnessed various vision applications based on local descriptors in the past decade. After 10 years' development, there are many outstanding methods proposed in the area of local image description that are competent to outperform SIFT in many applications.

This book is specialized in local image descriptors, covering the classical methods and the state-of-the-art methods as well as the burgeoning research topics on this area. It mainly comprises three parts. The first part introduces the classical local descriptors which are widely used in the literature. The second part is focused on the state of the art, i.e., recently developed more robust methods based on intensity orders, and some burgeoning methods that could be a promising future research direction. The third part gives some hands-on exemplar applications of local descriptors. Therefore, by reading this book, readers can rapidly know what a local image descriptor is and what it can do. As many local descriptors with different properties are introduced in the book, along with their advantages and disadvantages, it will be beneficial to researchers and practitioners who are searching for solutions for their specific applications or problems.

The book offers a rich blend of theory and practice. It is suitable for graduates, researchers, and practitioners interested in computer vision both as a learning text and as a reference book.

I thank Prof. Pascal Fua in École Polytechnique Fédérale de Lausanne (EPFL) for hosting me as a visiting scholar in his lab. Most parts of this book were completed during this time. It was a happy time to conduct research there. I also thank Prof. Zhanyi Hu in Institute of Automation, Chinese Academy of Sciences (CASIA), for bringing me to the world of computer vision, and for his valuable suggestions on my research and career. Special thanks to Prof. Chunhong Pan in

CASIA for always supporting me in exploring the unknown scientific world in his research group. Finally, thanks to the publication team of SpringerBriefs for its assistance.

The writing of this book is supported by the National Natural Science Foundation of China (Grant No. 61203277,61272394), Beijing Natural Science Foundation (Grant No. 4142057), and the Chinese Scholarship Council.

Lausanne, Switzerland   Bin Fan
August 2015

Contents

Chapter 1
Introduction

Local image descriptor is a kind of vector (either in float type or binary type) used as the signature of a local image. The aim of this representation is to make the local image as distinctive as possible while maintaining robustness to various kinds of image transformations, both photometric and geometric ones, including viewpoint changes (out-plane rotation), scale changes, in-plane rotation, image blur, noise, illumination, etc. By achieving these characteristics, one can easily establish correspondences among images of the same scene taken from different positions, or among similar images. Many computer vision applications are then built upon these correspondences, such as 3D reconstruction [1], image stitch [16], object/instance recognition [10] and so on [13, 15, 22].

However, designing an excellent local image descriptor which is highly discriminative and robust to various image transformations is not an easy job. In fact, the discriminative ability and the robustness are two contradictory factors of a local descriptor, which cannot be well taken care of at the same time. One extreme case is that we can use the intensities of all pixels in a local image as its descriptor. It is so distinctive that even a slight change of the local image will result in a large difference between their descriptors. So it is not robust at all. On the other end, if we use a statistic (such as mean value) to represent the local image, it is very robust to many transformations, but it only has a very low discriminative ability. As a result, the aim of research in this area is to design different methods to tradeoff between discriminative ability and robustness.

Scale invariant feature transform (SIFT) [10] is a milestone work in the area of local image description. It has been widely used in many visual applications described before, and largely inspires many local image descriptors proposed later in this area. Histogram of oriented gradient (HoG) [5] that is widely used in pedestrian detection is one example. Another example is the speeded up robust features (SURF) [3], which approximates SIFT by using the integral image technique to speedup its computation while keeping comparable matching performance. SURF is an alternate to SIFT in many applications which require quick process but can tolerate a bit worse matching performance than SIFT. This is because that although SURF could achieve

© Springer-Verlag Berlin Heidelberg 2015
B. Fan et al., *Local Image Descriptor: Modern Approaches*,
SpringerBriefs in Computer Science, DOI 10.1007/978-3-662-49173-7_1

a comparable or even better performance than SIFT in the benchmark dataset [11], it is sometimes inferior to SIFT in real cases.

It has been over one decade since SIFT was proposed, and lots of approaches have been proposed. Meanwhile, some new techniques and insights about designing better local image descriptor are emerging. Therefore, this book aims to give an in-time summarization of the past achievements as well as to introduce some emerging but burgeoning techniques. We also introduce several typical applications in which local image descriptor plays a key role. Finally, we would like to give some suggestions to readers, who want to conduct research on this area by describing the useful evaluation protocols and benchmark datasets, as well as summarize the existing work and list some possible directions for the future work.

The remaining of this book is organized as follows:

- Chapter 2 introduces some classical local descriptors which have been widely used in the computer vision community. These descriptors include SIFT [10] and SURF [3] that have a profound influence not only on wide-baseline image matching, but also on many high-level computer vision applications, such as image classification and retrieval. Meanwhile, the widely used local binary pattern (LBP) [12] and its variants are also introduced in this chapter.

- Chapter 3 elaborates a series of recently proposed methods based on intensity order for feature description. While gradient orientation distribution has shown its effectiveness in feature description, intensity is largely ignored by the research community due to its sensitiveness to illumination changes. However, recent works (e.g., local intensity order pattern (LIOP) [19], multisupport region order-based gradient histogram (MROGH) [7], ordinal and spatial information of regional invariants (OSRI) [21]) bring back of our attention to it. By using intensity orders, some approaches have achieved better performance than SIFT in terms of not only more discriminative power but also more robustness and compactness. This chapter will describe this kind of approach.

- Chapter 4 introduces binary descriptors, which are becoming popular in recent years due to their potential in large-scale and real-time applications. These binary descriptors include binary robust independent element features (BRIEF) [4], oriented FAST and rotated BRIEF (ORB) [14], binary robust and invariant scalable keypoints (BRISK) [8], fast retina keypoint (FEARK) [2], fast robust invariant feature (FRIF) [20] and some learning-based ones [6, 9, 17, 18].

- Chapter 5 gives instructions on how to use local image descriptors for different practical computer vision applications, including 3D reconstruction, object recognition, image search, and simultaneous localization and mapping (SLAM). A typical implementation for each of these applications is elaborated in this chapter so that readers can see how local image descriptors play a key role in computer vision.

- Chapter 6 finally concludes this book by giving some suggestions to the potential researchers in this area. These suggestions include popular used benchmark datasets and the standard evaluation protocols. Moreover, based on a summarization of existing work in this area, we would discuss some potential directions for future work.

References

1. Agarwal, S., Snavely, N., Simon, I., Seitz, S., Szeliski, R.: Building Rome in a day. In: International Conference on Computer Vision, pp. 72–79 (2009)
2. Alahi, A., Ortiz, R., Vandergheynst, P.: FREAK: Fast retina keypoint. In: IEEE Conference on Computer Vision and Pattern Recognition, pp. 510–517 (2012)
3. Bay, H., Ess, A., Tuytelaars, T., Gool, L.V.: SURF: speeded up robust features. Comput. Vis. Image Underst. **110**(3), 346–359 (2008)
4. Calonder, M., Lepetit, V., Ozuysal, M., Trzcinski, T., Strecha, C., Fua, P.: BRIEF: computing a local binary descriptor very fast. IEEE Trans. Pattern Anal. Mach. Intell. **33**(7), 1281–1298 (2012)
5. Dalal, N., Triggs, B.: Histograms of oriented gradients for human detection. In: IEEE Conference on Computer Vision and Pattern Recognition, pp. 886–893 (2005)
6. Fan, B., Kong, Q., Trzcinski, T., Wang, Z., Pan, C., Fua, P.: Receptive fields selection for binary feature description. IEEE Trans. Image Process. **23**(6), 2583–2595 (2014)
7. Fan, B., Wu, F., Hu, Z.: Rotationally invariant descriptors using intensity order pooling. IEEE Trans. Pattern Anal. Mach. Intell. **34**(10), 2031–2045 (2012)
8. Leutenegger, S., Chli, M., Siegwart, R.: BRISK: Binary robust invariant scalable keypoints. In: International Conference on Computer Vision, pp. 2548–2555 (2011)
9. Liu, W., Wang, J., Ji, R., Jiang, Y.G., Chang, S.F.: Supervised hashing with kernels. In: IEEE Conference on Computer Vision and Pattern Recognition, pp. 2074–2081 (2012)
10. Lowe, D.: Distinctive image features from scale-invariant keypoints. Int. J. Comput. Vis. **60**(2), 91–110 (2004)
11. Mikolajczyk, K., Schmid, C.: A performance evaluation of local descriptors. IEEE Trans. Pattern Anal. Mach. Intell. **27**(10), 1615–1630 (2005)
12. Ojala, T., Pietikainen, M., Harwood, D.: A comparative study of texture measures with classification based on feature distributions. Pattern Recogn. **29**, 51–59 (1996)
13. Philbin, J., Chum, O., Isard, M., Sivic, J., Zisserman, A.: Object retrieval with large vocabularies and fast spatial matching. In: IEEE Conference on Computer Vision and Pattern Recognition, pp. 1–8 (2007)
14. Rublee, E., Rabaud, V., Konolige, K., Bradski, G.: ORB: An efficient alternative to SIFT or SURF. In: International Conference on Computer Vision, pp. 2564–2571 (2011)
15. Sironi, A., Tekin, B., Rigamonti, R., Lepetit, V., Fua, P.: Learning separable filters. IEEE Trans. Pattern Anal. Mach. Intell. **37**(1), 94–106 (2015)
16. Szeliski, R.: Image alignment and stitching: a tutorial. Found. Trends Comput. Graph. Vis. **2**, 1–104 (2006)
17. Trzcinski, T., Christoudias, M., Fua, P., Lepetit, V.: Boosting binary keypoint descriptors. In: IEEE Conference on Computer Vision and Pattern Recognition, pp. 2874–2881 (2013)
18. Trzcinski, T., Lepetit, V.: Efficient discriminative projections for compact binary descriptors. In: European Conference on Computer Vision, pp. 228–242 (2012)
19. Wang, Z., Fan, B., Wu, F.: Local intensity order pattern for feature description. In: International Conference on Computer Vision, pp. 603–610 (2011)
20. Wang, Z., Fan, B., Wu, F.: FRIF: Fast robust invariant feature. In: British Machine Vision Conference (2013)
21. Xu, X., Tian, L., Feng, J., Zhou, J.: OSRI: a rotationally invariant binary descriptor. IEEE Trans. Image Process. **23**(7), 2983–2995 (2014)
22. Zhang, J., Marszalek, M., Lazebnik, S., Schmid, C.: Local features and kernels for classification of texture and object categories: a comprehensive study. Int. J. Comput. Vis. **73**(2), 213–238 (2007)

Chapter 2
Classical Local Descriptors

Abstract Classical local descriptors refer to those were proposed many years ago but have a profound influence on the development of local image description as well as related applications. Scale-Invariant Feature Transform (SIFT) and Speeded Up Robust Feature (SURF) are the two widely used descriptors in computer vision. Especially for SIFT, it is an extremely popular solution to various applications, ranging from object recognition, image retrieval, to structure from motion, etc. While for SURF, it is a first and predominant choice for those applications requiring fast or near real-time image matching until the very recent flourish of binary descriptors. Another classical local feature is Local Binary Pattern (LBP) proposed in the 1990s. Along with many variants, LBP has been ubiquitous in texture classification and many face-related tasks, e.g., face recognition, face detection, and facial expression recognition. Because of their popularity, we choose to introduce them in detail in this chapter.

Keywords SIFT · SURF · LBP · Scale space representation · Float type descriptor

2.1 Scale-Invariant Feature Transform (SIFT)

Scale-Invariant Feature Transform (SIFT) [9] is one of the most successful local descriptors, and it has been widely used in various vision tasks, such as image classification, image retrieval, image registration, pose estimation, to name a few. Basically, SIFT includes both feature detection and feature description. According to the context and application, sometimes SIFT only refers to its method for feature description, i.e., SIFT feature descriptor. For clarity, the term of "SIFT keypoint" is usually used to indicate its detected feature.

Generally speaking, SIFT is a scale-invariant method, and at the same time keeps robustness to many other image transformations, including in-plane rotation, small-to-medium viewpoint changes (caused by out-plane rotation of camera), image blur, illumination, and noise. The scale invariance and its robustness to image rotation are achieved by SIFT feature detector, which can detect keypoints with their scales and reference orientations. While the robustness to other transformations is obtained by the way of constructing a SIFT descriptor.

© Springer-Verlag Berlin Heidelberg 2015
B. Fan et al., *Local Image Descriptor: Modern Approaches*,
SpringerBriefs in Computer Science, DOI 10.1007/978-3-662-49173-7_2

2.1.1 Scale Space Representation in SIFT

In order to achieve scale invariance, SIFT operates on a Gaussian scale space to detect keypoints and construct their local descriptors. Gaussian scale space of an input image is defined as a series of images obtained by convolving the input image with gradually increased Gaussian variances. Given an input image $I(x, y)$, its Gaussian convolved image can be represented by:

$$L(x, y, \sigma) = I(x, y) * G(\sigma) \tag{2.1}$$

where $G(\sigma)$ denotes a Gaussian filter with the standard variance of σ. Thus, a set of convolved images $\{L(x, y, \sigma_i), i = 1, 2, \ldots, n\}$ is used to denote the Gaussian scale space of the image I. In the implementation of SIFT, σ is increased by a constant factor k, i.e., $\sigma_{i+1} = k\sigma_i$.

In order to detect keypoints which are robust to scale changes and with a high repeatability, SIFT takes the extrema in a DoG (Difference of Gaussian) scale space as the initial keypoints, and then with some refinement and adjustment to determine the final keypoints (will be described in the next section). For this purpose, a DoG scale space is constructed on the basis of the Gaussian scale space, by subtracting adjacent image scales:

$$D(x, y, \sigma) = L(x, y, k\sigma) - L(x, y, \sigma) \tag{2.2}$$

The computation time of Gaussian convolution is positively related to the size of image as well as the size of used Gaussian kernel. Therefore, for efficiency, $L(\sigma_{i+1})$ is computed by convolving $L(\sigma_i)$ with $\sigma'_{i+1} = \sqrt{\sigma_{i+1}^2 - \sigma_i^2}$, instead of directly convolving I with σ_{i+1}. On the other hand, SIFT also uses an octave-based structure for scale space representation. More specifically, images in a scale space are divided into octaves, each of which doubles σ, i.e., scale. In each octave, it further divides the scale space into s layers, so, $k = 2^{1/s}$ as $k^s = 2$. As we will describe later, SIFT searches for extrema in the DoG scale space along three dimensions for keypoint detection. Therefore, it needs $s + 2$ DoG images to cover a complete octave. As shown in Fig. 2.1, the two additional layers are used for keypoint detection in the first and the last layer. Accordingly, $s + 3$ Gaussian blurred images are required to generate these $s + 2$ DoG images. After one octave has been processed, the $(s + 1)$th image in this octave is downsampled by a factor of 2 to generate the first image in the next octave. In this way, the whole octaves will cover a set of scales increased by a constant factor, as can be seen in Fig. 2.1.

According to several experiments, Lowe suggested to set $\sigma = 1.6$ [9]. Meanwhile, in order to get more stable keypoints, he also proposed to double the original image by a factor of 2 and use it to construct the first octave of the scale space.

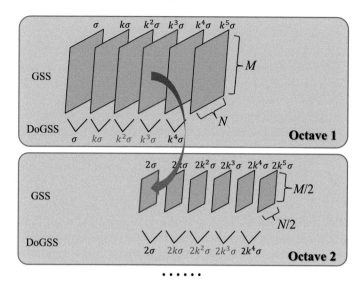

Fig. 2.1 The scale space representation implemented in SIFT when $s = 3$. DoG scale space (*DoGSS*) is generated by subtracting adjacent images in the Gaussian scale space (*GSS*). The *red* values indicate the scales that will be used for keypoint detection by 3D extrema search. To make these scales consistently differ by a factor of k, it has to generate $s + 2$ images in each octave of DoGSS and $s + 3$ images in GSS. See the text for details

2.1.2 Keypoint Detection

To detect scale-invariant keypoints, SIFT first searches for the local maxima and minima of $D(x, y, \sigma)$ by comparing each pixel to its 8 neighbors in the current layer and the 18 neighbors in the above and below layers. Then, non-maximum suppression is used to filter out those close enough but unstable local extrema, obtaining a set of points in discrete positions and some levels of predefined scales. The next step is to estimate the accurate positions (up to subpixels) and scales. Meanwhile, it is important to remove some keypoints with low contrasts and those poorly localized along edges, because both of these cases will result in unstable keypoints.

The accurate localization of a keypoint $X_0 = (x, y, \sigma)$ is obtained by fitting a 3D quadratic function around the local area of X_0 and taking the interpolated position of its extremum. To this end, we first have to shift the origin of the scale response function, i.e., DoG response, to X_0. Then, the Taylor expansion is applied to the shifted $D(x, y, \sigma)$:

$$D(X) = D(X_0) + X^T \frac{\partial D}{\partial X}(X_0) + \frac{1}{2} X^T \frac{\partial^2 D}{\partial X^2}(X_0)X \tag{2.3}$$

To get the extremum of $D(X)$, we can compute the derivative of $D(X)$ and set it to zero. In this way, we obtain the following equation:

$$\frac{\partial^2 D}{\partial X^2}(X_0)\Delta X = -\frac{\partial D}{\partial X}(X_0) \tag{2.4}$$

ΔX is the offset of the extreme point to the original point X_0, so the refined keypoint is localized at $X = X_0 + \Delta X$. It is worth to note that if the offset ΔX is larger than 0.5 in any dimension, it implies that the extremum lies closer to a neighboring point of X_0. In this case, X_0 is changed to this neighboring point and the above procedure of getting offset is repeated, until all the dimensions in the offset are less than 0.5.

Substituting $X = X_0 + \Delta X$ into Eq. (2.3), we can obtain its DoG value:

$$D(X) = D(X_0) + \frac{1}{2}\Delta X^T \frac{\partial D}{\partial X}(X_0) \tag{2.5}$$

The extremum with a value of $|D(X)|$ less than 0.03 (the pixel value is assumed in the range of [0,1]) is discarded due to its low contrast (sensitive to noise).

Since the DoG function will have a strong response along edges, this kind of extremum is unstable to noise and usually has a large localization error. Meanwhile, points localized along the edges usually have less distinctive local appearance, which will make extracting discriminative descriptors for them a difficult task. For these reasons, they have to be discarded.

Except for the extreme response in the DoG scale space, these kind of points also have a large principal curvature along an edge and with a small one along the prependicular direction. These two curvatures are proportional to the eigenvalues of a Hessian matrix H, which is computed at the scale and location of the keypoint as:

$$H = \begin{bmatrix} Dxx & Dxy \\ Dxy & Dyy \end{bmatrix} \tag{2.6}$$

where the derivatives Dxx, Dxy, Dyy are computed by taking the differences of neighboring sample points in the scale space.

Directly computing the eigenvalues of H is a bit slow, fortunately, here we only concern the ratio of its two eigenvalues, but not the concrete eigenvalues. Suppose the two eigenvalues are both positives and as λ and $r\lambda$ with $r \geq 1$, they satisfy:

$$tr(H) = \lambda + r\lambda = (1 + r)\lambda \tag{2.7}$$

$$Det(H) = \lambda \times r\lambda = r\lambda^2 \tag{2.8}$$

We can further obtain:

$$\frac{tr(H)^2}{Det(H)} = \frac{(r + 1)^2}{r} \tag{2.9}$$

Since $r \geq 1$, $\frac{tr(H)^2}{Det(H)}$ is monotonic increased along with r. As a result, we just need to set a threshold on $\frac{tr(H)^2}{Det(H)}$ to discard the point with large r, which corresponds to a large principal curvature and a small one. In the implementation of SIFT, r is set to be 10. In case that $Det(H)$ is negative (it will have a negative eigenvalue), the keypoint is discarded as not being an extremum, but this rarely happens.

The final step for keypoint detection is to assign an orientation to each keypoint. Note that this step is optional. If the task does not have to deal with images with rotations, this step can be skipped and obtain a better performance both in efficiency and accuracy. Otherwise, this step is useful to achieve rotation invariance. The orientation of a keypoint is computed from a circular neighborhood depending on its scale. Specifically, given a keypoint (x, y, σ), we first take out the Gaussian blurred image closest to σ from the scale space. All the following operations are conducted in this image so as to be scale invariant. Then, a histogram of gradient orientations (360 degree is quantized to 36 bins) is computed from a local circular region around the keypoint. The radius of this circular region is set to be 4.5σ. Besides the gradient magnitude of each sample point in this region, it is also weighted by a Gaussian function with 1.5σ as standard variance when adding it to the histogram. Finally, the orientation corresponding to the highest peak in this histogram is taken as the orientation of this keypoint. For other peaks that are within 80 % of the highest peak, their corresponding orientations are also taken as the orientations of the keypoint. Therefore, for one keypoint, it may split into several keypoints, which differ only by their orientations. It is worth to point out that when computing the orientation corresponding to a peak, a parabola is fitted to the 3 histogram bins centered at the peak to interpolate the peak position for better accuracy.

2.1.3 Feature Description

In the keypoint detection, each keypoint is detected along with its position, scale, and orientation. These parameters can be used to construct a local descriptor to describe this keypoint in a scale and rotation-invariant manner. Briefly speaking, as shown in Fig. 2.2, SIFT descriptor is constructed by dividing the local region defined by these parameters into 4×4 grids, then computing histograms of gradient orientations in these grids, and finally concatenating these histograms together which is further normalized to an unit vector as the descriptor.

First, similar to the computation of keypoint orientation, we have to take out the Gaussian blurred image in the scale space according to the scale of the keypoint. SIFT descriptor is constructed in this image to assure the scale invariance. Then, a local region with 16×16 sample points around the keypoint location is taken out from the image according to the keypoint scale σ. For each sample point, its gradient magnitude and orientation are computed. Note that to achieve rotation invariance, the coordinates and gradient orientations of these sample points are rotated relatively to the keypoint orientation. A Gaussian weighting function with standard variance as $1.5W$ (W is the width of the local region) is used to weight the magnitude of each sample point in order to put more emphasize on those sample points near to the keypoint.

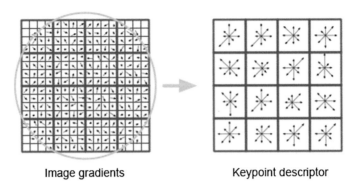

Image gradients   Keypoint descriptor

Fig. 2.2 SIFT descriptor is computed by accumulating and concatenating gradient orientation distributions in 4×4 spatial grids. Gradient orientation is weighted by its magnitude and a Gaussian weighting function centered at the keypoint. Reprinted from Lowe [9], with kind permission from Springer Science+Business Media

Meanwhile, in order to be robust to shift in these sample points as well as encoding some spatial information to improve the distinctiveness, the 16×16 local region is further divided into 4×4 grids. In each grid, a histogram of gradient orientations is computed on the basis of gradient magnitudes and Gaussian weights. All histograms are concatenated together to form a 128-dimensional descriptor. To handle sudden illumination changes, a two-step normalization is used. The 128 descriptor is first normalized to unit length. Then any element larger than 0.2 is clipped to 0.2. The clipped vector is renormalized to unit length as the final SIFT descriptor.

From the above procedure, we can see that SIFT actually accumulates a 3D histogram of spatial locations and gradient orientations, weighted by a Gaussian function and gradient magnitude. To improve its robustness and avoid boundary effects, soft assignment is used. In this way, a sample point contributes to 8 neighboring bins in the 128-dimensional SIFT descriptor according to its distance to the center of each bin.

It is worth to point out that the famous Histograms of Oriented Gradients (HoG) proposed by Dalal and Triggs [4] for pedestrian detection shares a similar basic idea to SIFT descriptor. Both of them resort to accumulate oriented gradient responses, which are weighted by gradient magnitude, on different spatial areas in the described region. The difference is that HoG uses much more overlapping cells to collect histograms of oriented gradients, which are normalized according to the 'energy' in a larger region (block). The HoG detection window/described region is divided into many blocks to obtain a discriminative representation. Nowadays, HoG has been a standard technique of feature extraction for object detection, not merely to pedestrian detection.

2.2 Speeded Up Robust Feature (SURF)

Although SIFT is discriminative and robust to many geometric and photometric transformations, it is slow to compute, which limits its application to some extent. To alleviate this problem, Bay et al. [2] proposed a fast alternative to SIFT by modifying SIFT to make it adaptive to integral image, which can be computed very fast. Their method is called Speeded Up Robust Feature (SURF). Its algorithmic pipeline is similar to that of SIFT, which contains mainly three steps: (1) scale space representation of the input image; (2) detect SURF keypoints (interest points) in the scale space; (3) assign orientations to keypoints and construct their SURF descriptors. We will elaborate each of these steps in the following sections.

2.2.1 Integral Image

Before formally introducing these algorithmic steps of SURF, we start with a brief introduction of the integral image technique, which is at the core of SURF. By definition, the entry of an integral image I_Σ at a location (x, y) is the sum of all pixels in the input image I within a rectangular region formed by the origin (left top of an image) and (x, y). Therefore, given an image I of size $m \times n$, its integral image I_Σ can be computed as:

$$I_\Sigma(x, y) = \sum_{u=0}^{x} \sum_{v=0}^{y} I(u, v)$$

The advantage of integral image lies in the fast computation of the sum of the intensities over any upright, rectangular region. It can be shown that once the integral image has been computed, for any upright, rectangular region, it only requires three additions to obtain its summed intensities, no matter what the size of the region is. This is extremely useful when one has to frequently obtain intensity sums over regions and has to operate on large regions, which are the cases that SURF faces.

2.2.2 Scale Space Representation in SURF

In order to detect interest points along with different scales, one has to resort to a scale space representation of the input image. Usually, scale space is implemented as an image pyramid as SIFT does [9], in which the input image is repeatedly smoothed with a Gaussian kernel and then subsampled to obtain a higher level of the pyramid. Different from this usual strategy by iteratively reducing the image size, SURF proposes to obtain a scale space representation of the input image by repeatedly increasing the filter size, as shown in Fig. 2.3.

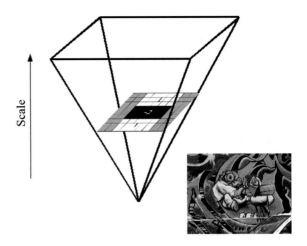

Besides the scale normalized Laplacian of Gaussian (LoG) approximated by the Difference of Gaussian (DoG) used in SIFT, the determinant of Hessian matrix is another popular measure for detecting scale-invariant interest points. SURF's interest point detector is based on the computation of such determinant, but with some approximation so as to be computed very fast. Mathematically, the Hessian matrix of a point x in image I at scale σ can be computed by:

$$H(x, \sigma) = \begin{bmatrix} L_{xx}(x, \sigma) & L_{xy}(x, \sigma) \\ L_{xy}(x, \sigma) & L_{yy}(x, \sigma) \end{bmatrix}$$

where $L_{xx}(x, \sigma)$ is the convolution of the second-order Gaussian derivative with image I in x, and σ is the standard variance of the Gaussian. Similarly for $L_{xy}(x, \sigma)$ and $L_{yy}(x, \sigma)$.

In order to use the integral image to efficiently compute the Hessian responses, SURF uses filters consisted by several box filters to approximate the second-order Gaussian derivatives as shown in Fig. 2.4. As the convolution of these box filters to image can be computed with only several additions based on the integral image, computing the approximated Hessian matrix is extremely fast. Formally, the approximated Hessian matrix $\hat{H}(x, \sigma)$ is defined by:

$$\hat{H}(x, \sigma) = \begin{bmatrix} D_{xx}(x, \sigma) & D_{xy}(x, \sigma) \\ D_{xy}(x, \sigma) & D_{yy}(x, \sigma) \end{bmatrix}$$

where $D_{xx}(x, \sigma)$, $D_{yy}(x, \sigma)$ and $D_{xy}(x, \sigma)$ are the convolutions of the approximated filters with image I respectively.

The determinant of Hessian matrix can be served as the response of a blob point, that is, $R(x, \sigma) = L_{xx}L_{yy} - L_{xy}^2 \approx D_{xx}D_{yy} - (0.9D_{xy}^2)$. In order to guarantee a constant Frobenius norm of any filter size, $R(x)$ is normalized with the corresponding filter size. This is important for scale space analysis as it prevents the reduction of filter

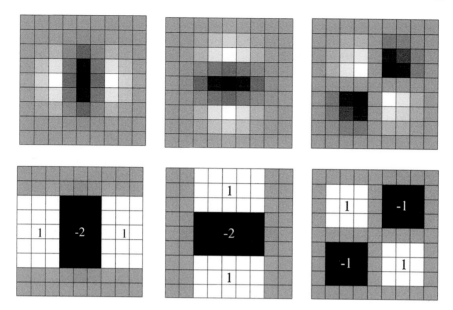

Fig. 2.4 Approximation of Gaussian second-order partial derivatives by *box filters*. From *left* to *right* are *Lxx*, *Lyy*, and *Lxy*. The approximated *box filters* are listed below their original ones. Reprinted from Bay et al. [3], with kind permission from Springer Science+Business Media

response at larger scales. Based on this measurement, interest points are detected across scales by non-maximum suppression which will be described in the next section. As can be seen, only $D_{xx}(x, \sigma)$, $D_{yy}(x, \sigma)$, and $D_{xy}(x, \sigma)$ are related to the interest point detection, thus three scale spaces are actually generated. One is for $D_{xx}(x, \sigma)$, and the other two for $D_{yy}(x, \sigma)$ and $D_{xy}(x, \sigma)$.

Similar to the octave structure utilized in SIFT, SURF also adapts this structure to represent the scale space. Specifically, each octave includes a scaling factor of 2, and contains several levels, each of which corresponds to an convolved image by a predefined filter size related to the scale of this level. The filter sizes of neighboring scales differ in a constant factor within an octave, and this size difference is doubled for neighboring octaves. As explained before, SURF uses box filters to approximate the second-order Gaussian derivatives. 9×9 is the minimal box filter size for this approximation (corresponding to a Gaussian with $\sigma = 1.2$), so it serves as the minimal scale in the scale space. As shown in Fig. 2.4, there are three parts in D_{xx} and D_{yy}. In order to assure that the total filter size is uneven, the minimal size that can be increased by each part is 2 for the two successive scales. As a result, it is 6 for the whole filter. Therefore, in the first octave, the filter sizes are 9, 15, 21, ... In the following step of finding extreme points in the scale space, it can be seen that it requires two additional neighboring levels to detect interest points in a certain level. Therefore, the first level and the last level in each octave are only for auxiliary purpose. Meanwhile, due to the interpolation in scale space for refining an interest point's scale, the smallest scale in the first octave is $\frac{(9+15)}{2} \times \frac{1.2}{9} = 1.6$. Since an octave includes a scaling factor of 2, therefore, the largest scale in the first octave is 3.2, which corresponds to a filter size of 24, so the last useful level for interest point detection is 21 (because $\frac{(21+27)}{2} = 24$). Similarly, the filter sizes in the second octave are 15, 27, 39, 51; in the third octave are 27, 51, 75, 99, until the input image size is no longer larger than the filter size. As can be seen, the octaves in this scale space representation are overlapped to cover all the possible scales seamlessly.

From the above structure of the scale space, it is obvious that the sampling of scales is quite crude. For example, in the first two levels of the first octave, the scale change is $15/9 = 1.67$. Therefore, SURF also supplies a strategy for obtaining a scale space representation with finer sampling scales at the cost of a little more computational time. This strategy starts by doubling the input image using linear interpolation. Then, in the first octave, its first level is 15×15, instead of 9×9 in the original version. The filter sizes are 21, 27, 33, 39 in the remaining levels of the first octave. The remaining things are similar to those in the original version. The second octave starts with 27 and increased by a factor of 12, and so on for the third octave, the fourth octave, etc. In this implementation of the scale space, it can be found that the scale change is $21/15 = 1.4$, smaller than 1.67. Meanwhile, the finest scale that can be obtained by quadratic interpolation is $\frac{(15+21)}{2} \times \frac{1.2}{9} \times \frac{1}{2} = 1.2$.

2.2.3 Scale-Invariant Interest Point Detection

Interest points are localized by applying a non-maximum suppression of $R(x, \sigma)$ in $3 \times 3 \times 3$ neighborhood of both spatial and scale spaces. The fast non-maximum suppression technique described in [10] is used in SURF. The basic idea is the two local maxima are separated by at least r pixels in each dimension, where r is the neighborhood radius used for non-maximum suppression. Therefore, there is no need to check all the pixels.

As the position defined by the spatial grid and the crude sampling of scales is unstable, it is necessary to use an additional procedure to refine the location. This is achieved by interpolation through fitting a paraboloid over the space and scale that is identical to SIFT. Please refer to Sect. 2.1 for the details. After this procedure, maxima with subpixel/subscale accuracy are obtained, and are taken as the detected interest points.

2.2.4 Orientation Assignment and Descriptor Construction

In order to make the SURF descriptor invariant to image rotation, a reproducible orientation is first computed based on the information from a circular region around the interest point. Then, a square region aligned to the computed orientation is constructed. Finally, SURF descriptor is extracted from this square region.

Fig. 2.5 The Haar wavelet filters used for computing responses in x (*left*) and y (*right*) directions at scale s. Reprinted from Bay et al. [2], with permission from Elsevier

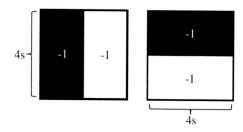

To compute a reproducible orientation for each interest point, a circular neighborhood of radius $6s$ around the interest point is used, where s is the scale of the interest point. For each sampling point (rounded to be integer in order to use integral images) in this region, the Haar wavelet responses in x and y directions are calculated, which are denoted by dx and dy respectively. In order to keep scale invariance, the sampling step is set to be s. Meanwhile, the size of the Haar wavelet is also scale dependent and set to be $4s$, as illustrated in Fig. 2.5. By using integral images, only six operations are needed for computing the response in x/y direction at any scale. To give a more emphasis on the central sampling points, a Gaussian ($\sigma = 2s$) weighting function is applied to these Haar wavelet responses. Then, all these Gaussian weighted responses are mapped to a 2D space with x direction response as abscissa and y direction response as ordinate. A sliding orientation window of size $\pi/3$ is used to sum all the points to get a local orientation vector (cf. Fig. 2.6). Finally, the longest orientation vector across all sliding windows is taken as the orientation of the interest point.

In order to extract the SURF descriptor for an interest point, it has to construct a square region centered in the interest point and aligned to its orientation. The size of this square region is set to be $20s$ with a sampling step of s so as to obtain scale invariance. The square region is then regularly splitted into 4×4 subregions to keep

Fig. 2.6 A sliding orientation window is used for accumulating the weighted responses in x and y directions. The longest accumulated vector across all sliding windows is taken as the orientation of the interest point. Reprinted from Bay et al. [2], with permission from Elsevier

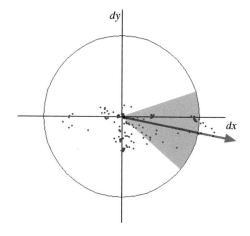

the important spatial information for distinctiveness. For each sample point in this squared region, its Haar wavelet responses in horizontal and vertical directions (dx and dy) are computed. Note that the 'horizontal' and 'vertical' are defined according to the orientation of the interest point. Different from the Haar wavelets used in orientation assignment, here the filter size is set to be $2s$. For efficiency, instead of rotating image and computing these Haar wavelet responses, they are first computed in the unrotated image and then rotated according to the interest point's orientation. They are then mapped to a 4-dimensional vector to encode information about the polarity of the intensity changes, i.e., $(dx, |dx|, dy, |dy|)$. Finally, these 4-dimensional vectors are summed up over each subregion, weighted by a Gaussian function ($\sigma = 3.3s$) centered at the interest point. All the accumulated vectors in all the 16 subregions are concatenated together to form the SURF descriptor (64 dimension), which is normalized to be unit length to achieve invariance to contrast changes. Using Gaussian function to weight the responses of sample points is to increase the robustness toward localization error and geometric deformation.

To further improve the descriptor's discriminative ability, an alternative version of SURF descriptor is to map the Haar wavelet responses to a 8-dimensional vector: $((dx, |dx|)_{dy>0}, (dx, |dx|)_{dy\leq0}, (dy, |dy|)_{dx>0}, (dy, |dy|)_{dx\leq0}) \in R^8$, where $(dy, |dy|)_{dx>0}$ means it is only valid when $dx > 0$, otherwise, it is set to $(0, 0)$. Similarly for other terms. This alternative version has a dimension of 128. It is more distinctive and only a bit slower to compute, but slower to match and requires two times of storage due to its high dimensionality.

2.3 Local Binary Pattern and Its Variants

Another very popular and well-known local feature is the family of Local Binary Pattern (LBP). Since the first basic LBP has been introduced in 1990s, LBP methodology has developed a lot in the past two decades, ranging from extensions, related theories, to various new applications.

In the beginning, LBP [11] was proposed to describe texture, which could be characterized by a nonuniform distribution of intensities or colors, with applications to texture classification and segmentation. Due to its good performance and computational simplicity, LBP rapidly gained its popularity in the computer vision community and has become a widely used operator for image processing in real world applications, not limited to texture-related applications.

By applying LBP operator to an image, each pixel is denoted by an integer label (e.g., 256 different labels in the original LBP with 3×3 neighborhood configuration) which is robust to monotonic illumination change. Each of these labels is called a LBP pattern. In the original version of LBP [11], the LBP pattern for a pixel is computed by comparing each of its neighboring pixel in a 3×3 area to the central pixel about their intensities, as shown in Fig. 2.7. Such a comparison will result in

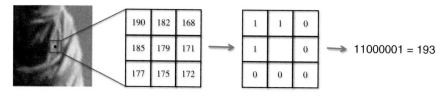

Fig. 2.7 Illustration of LBP computation for a pixel

a bit string with 8 elements, therefore, $2^8 = 256$ different possible labels in total. Mathematically, a more *generic definition of LBP* is given in the following [12]:

$$LBP_{R,N}(x) = \sum_{i=0}^{N-1} sign(I(x_i) - I(x))2^i \qquad (2.10)$$

where $sign(x)$ is the sign function that outputs 1 when input is larger than 0, otherwise outputs 0. R defines a circular neighborhood of the pixel x with radius R, and N denotes the number of regularly sampling points on this circle used for LBP computation. In any case that a sampling point is not located in a discrete pixel, the bilinear interpolation is used to get its intensity.

Based on experimental results, Ojala et al. [12] proposed uniform patterns of LBP. Based on the definition of LBP pattern, they further defined an uniformity measure of a pattern as the number of bitwise transitions from 0 to 1 or from 1 to 0 in its binary representation. Note that in this definition, a pattern is considered circularly. The uniformity measure can be formulated as:

$$U(LBP_{R,N}) = \sum_{i=1}^{N-1} |b_{i+1} - b_i| + |b_1 - b_N| \qquad (2.11)$$

in which b_i is the ith bit of the LBP bit string.

According to this uniformity measure, Ojala et al. defined the LBP patterns whose uniformity measures are no larger than 2 as the *uniform patterns*: $LBP_{R,N}^u = \{LBP_{R,N}|U(LBP_{R,N}) \leq 2\}$. For N bits LBP pattern, there are $N(N-1)+2$ uniform patterns. Usually, for the remaining nonuniform patterns, they are considered together as a single label (pattern). Therefore, with the uniform patterns, histogram of LBP can be reduced from 2^N bins to $N(N-1)+3$ bins, largely reducing the dimension used for feature description. Meanwhile, uniform patterns are found to be more stable and dominant in natural images. For example, nearly 90 % of all patterns are uniform patterns when using $(R = 1, N = 8)$ LBP neighborhood according to Ojala et al. experiments with texture images. Similar statistical result is also observed in facial images [1].

To achieve a rotation-invariant representation, a LBP pattern is circularly shifted into its minimum integer value [14], as following:

$$LBP_{R,N}^{ri} = \min_{i \in [1,N]} shift(LBP_{R,N}, i) \qquad (2.12)$$

where $shift(LBP_{R,N}, i)$ indicates the right-shifted operation (in a circular way) to $LBP_{R,N}$ by i bits. The pattern $LBP_{R,N}^{ri}$ corresponding to this minimum integer value is defined as the *rotation-invariant LBP*. In case of $N = 8$, there are 36 rotation-invariant LBPs. We can see that rotation-invariant LBP actually maps a set of LBP patterns into a single one, thus the discriminative power may be reduced. Due to the definition of $LBP_{R,N}$ and $LBP_{R,N}^{ri}$, theoretically, such a rotation invariance is only available by angles $2\pi \times i/N, i = 1, \ldots, N - 1$. However, in practice, it is very robust by any angle.

In the set of uniform patterns, besides the patterns with all 1 s and all 0s, it contains $N - 1$ groups of patterns. Each group contains N patterns with i ($1 \leq i < N$) 1s, all of which only differ by rotation. Therefore, each group actually corresponds to one pattern if we do not consider rotation. As a result, there are totally $N+1$ different such patterns, known as *rotation-invariant uniform patterns*. They can be formulated by:

$$LBP_{R,N}^{riu} = \left\{ \sum_{i=1}^{N} b_i | U(LBP_{R,N}) \leq 2 \right\} \qquad (2.13)$$

Similar to the case of uniform pattern, all the other patterns that do not belong to any of the rotation-invariant uniform patterns are considered as a single pattern.

Many extensions of LBP have been proposed to either improve its robustness and discriminative power or adapt it to new computer vision tasks. These variants include improvements on many parts of LBP, for example, incorporating other complementary feature into LBP, changing its method for thresholding and intensity comparison, extending with multiscale analysis, making it capable of dealing with color information, extending it to spatiotemporal area, etc. In this section, we will briefly describe some of these variants which we think are important in the development of LBP. For a comprehensive review and introduction of LBP variants, we refer the interested readers to [13].

Local Gabor Binary Patterns: Local Gabor Binary Patterns (LGBP) [17] is a very good local feature popularly used in face recognition. It effectively combines local and regional information by using Gabor filtering and LBP operator together. Specifically, a facial image is first filtered by a set of Gabor filters with different scales and orientations, in order to obtain rich appearance information over a board range of scales and orientations. Then, LBP operator is applied to each of these Gabor filtered images (only the magnitudes are used), and a set of histograms are obtained for spatial subregions divided from the input facial image for each Gabor filtered image. Finally, all the histograms are concatenated together as the LGBP feature. Its pipeline is depicted in Fig. 2.8. However, the disadvantage of this method is the high dimensionality of this kind of representation, for example, with 5 scales and 8 orientations, it results in a face representation that have 40 times larger dimensions than that of using the original LBP.

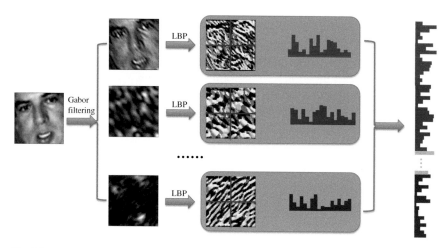

Fig. 2.8 The flowchart of computing LGBP

Multiscale Block Local Binary Pattern: Another widely used LBP variant in face recognition is Multiscale Block Local Binary Pattern (MB-LBP) [8]. It extends the original LBP to encode information from larger areas, so as to cover both micro- and macrostructures in facial images. Thus higher discriminative power is expected. The basic ideas of MB-LBP are to use the average intensity over a $s \times s$ subregion to replace the intensity of the central pixel/neighboring pixel in the original LBP. The size of s corresponds to the scale of MB-LBP. Usually, several scales of MB-LBP are used together, followed by the Adaboost algorithm [5] to select most discriminative features for face recognition. Figure 2.9 gives an example of using 3×3 subregions.

Another modification of LBP that MB-LBP proposed is to use a statistically effective set of uniform patterns obtained from training data. More specifically, a histogram of MB-LBP patterns is first obtained for each scale. Then, for each scale, the MB-LBP patterns correspond to the top N bins are obtained as the N uniform MB-LBP patterns and receive labels from 0 to $N - 1$. All the remaining patterns share a single label N. Since different scales are processed separately, the obtained

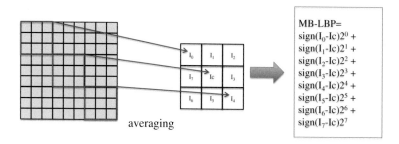

averaging

$$MB\text{-}LBP= \\ sign(I_0\text{-}Ic)2^0 + \\ sign(I_1\text{-}Ic)2^1 + \\ sign(I_2\text{-}Ic)2^2 + \\ sign(I_3\text{-}Ic)2^3 + \\ sign(I_4\text{-}Ic)2^4 + \\ sign(I_5\text{-}Ic)2^5 + \\ sign(I_6\text{-}Ic)2^6 + \\ sign(I_7\text{-}Ic)2^7$$

Fig. 2.9 Illustration of MB-LBP computation with 3×3 blocks

set of uniform MB-LBP patterns will have large redundance. The final set used for face recognition is selected by the Adaboost algorithm.

Local Ternary Pattern: To make LBP more robust to small changes/noise in intensity, which usually occurs in flat or near uniform image regions and shadow areas, Tan and Triggs [15] modified the binary pattern in LBP to a ternary pattern, obtaining the so-called Local Ternary Pattern (LTP). In LBP, it computes a two-value bit code (0 or 1) for each sampling point in the neighborhood by thresholding its intensity on that of the central pixel. While in LTP, it computes a three-value code $(-1, 0, 1)$ for each sampling point by thresholding on two intensities as follows:

$$s(x_i) = \begin{cases} 1, & I(x_i) \geq I(x) + t \\ 0, & I(x) - t \leq I(x_i) \leq I(x) + t \\ -1, & I(x_i) < I(x) - t \end{cases} \tag{2.14}$$

where $I(x)$ is the intensity of the central pixel, x_i is the ith sampling point in the neighborhood of x, and t is a predefined offset to generate two thresholds, usually set to be 5. All values of N sampling points are concatenated together to serve as the LTP code of the central pixel.

Intuitively, N sampling points could form a total of 3^N possible LTP codes. Such a large range will further make the histogram representation very sparse, which may degrade its discriminative power and make it sensitive to noise. For these reasons, the N three value codes $s(x_i), i = 1, \ldots, N$ are divided into two sets according to their signs, obtaining two local binary patterns, as shown in Fig. 2.10. These two parts are used separately to obtain representations of the described region, e.g., histograms. These representations are finally concatenated as a single feature vector.

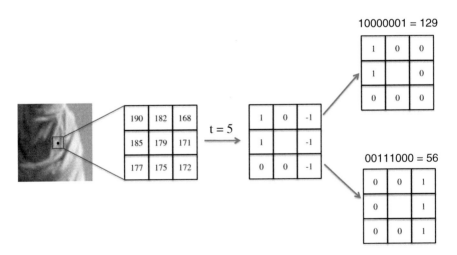

Fig. 2.10 Illustration of LTP computation for a pixel when $t = 5$

A drawback of LTP is that using a constant offset t to generate two thresholds makes the computed LTP code not invariant under scale change of intensities. Liao et al. [7] noticed this problem and proposed a Scale-Invariant LTP (SILTP) to address it. The basic idea of SILTP is very simple, i.e., replacing the offset t in LTP with a value proportional to the intensity of the central pixel. Meanwhile, to avoid splitting a ternary code into two binary ones, they used two bits to represent the obtained three values. Concatenating all the binary codes of sampling points then forms the SILTP representation for a pixel. Mathematically, the SILTP operator can be formulated as:

$$s_i(x_i) = \begin{cases} 01, & I(x_i) > (1+\tau)I(x) \\ 00, & (1-\tau)I(x) \le I(x_i) \le (1+\tau)I(x) \\ 10, & I(x_i) < (1-\tau)I(x) \end{cases} \tag{2.15}$$

where τ is a predefined scale factor, indicating how much of the central pixel's intensity can be tolerated. Apparently, SILTP operator is scale-invariant about intensities.

Center-Symmetric Local Binary Pattern: Although LBP has high discriminative power and good robustness to illumination change, its high dimensionality makes it not suitable for describing an interest region around a keypoint, for which a low-dimensional descriptor is usually required, for example, the 128-dimensional SIFT descriptor. Even the histogram of uniform LBP is still too long to be used in an interest region descriptor. One may argue that we can take the histogram of LBP in the entire interest region as the descriptor whose dimension is 256 if the original LBP is used. However, such method does not encode any spatial information in the descriptor which is very important on distinguishing different interest regions. Therefore, its discriminative ability is significantly reduced, making it useless in matching interest regions across different images.

In spite of the difficulties, the good performance of LBP against illumination changes makes it attractive to researchers working on the area of interest region description. Motivated by this, Heikkila et al. [6] modified LBP to have only 16 possible patterns in total when 8 neighborhood is used. In this case, it can be used in a feature description algorithm similar to SIFT and leads to a high-performance descriptor. The core idea of this modification is to compare intensities of the center-symmetric sampling points instead of compare intensities of the sampling point and the central pixel. Therefore, for a N neighborhood samplings, there are only $N/2$ bits generated, which can be further encoded into a $2^{N/2}$ dimensional histogram. The modified pattern is called Center-Symmetric Local Binary Pattern (CS-LBP). Moreover, since there may exist large portion of flat area in an interest region, it is necessary to adapt LBP to be robust to small intensity changes as this often occurs in flat area with noise. For this purpose, CS-LBP operator introduces a tolerant threshold on intensity comparison. To sum up, the CS-LBP operator of pixel x can be formulated as:

$$CS-LBP_{R,N}(x) = \sum_{i=0}^{N/2-1} sign(I(x_i) - I(x_{i+N/2}) - t)2^i \tag{2.16}$$

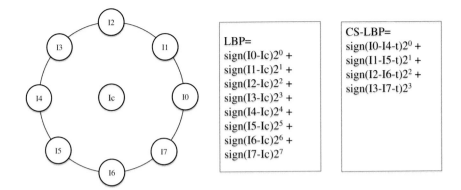

Fig. 2.11 A comparison of LBP operator and CS-LBP operator when 8 neighborhood samplings are used. Reprinted from Heikkila et al. [6], with kind permission from Springer Science+Business Media

The meanings of R, N and $sign(x)$ are identical to those in Eq. (2.10). t is a threshold balancing the tolerance to noise and discriminative power of CS-LBP. The bigger value the t is, the bigger turbulence to intensity it can resist. However, a small value of t is required to make CS-LBP discriminative. A typical setting of t is 3 in most cases. $I(x_i)$ and $I(x_{i+N/2})$ are intensities of two center-symmetric sampling points. Figure 2.11 depicts the difference of LBP and CS-LBP when $N = 8$.

The low-dimensional property of CS-LBP makes it suitable for interest region description by concatenating histograms in divided subregions like SIFT does. This is indeed the way that Heikkila et al. [6] did to construct a descriptor so as to combine strengths of SIFT and LBP. The resulting descriptor is called CS-LBP as well. The pipeline for constructing a CS-LBP descriptor is similar to that of SIFT, except for the following two differences:

(1) It does not have the feature weighting step, which assigns each pixel in the interest region a weight according to its gradient magnitude and a Gaussian function in SIFT. Omitting this step is supported by their experimental results reported in [6].
(2) When accumulating the 3D histogram of CS-LBP values and locations, a pixel is contributed to its 4 neighboring bins in spatial by using bilinear interpolation. While in SIFT, a pixel is contributed to its 8 neighboring bins by interpolation in both spatial and gradient orientation. Since CS-LBP is quantized by nature, it is not necessary to interpolate in this dimension when constructing CS-LBP descriptor.

Local Intensity Order Pattern: To fully explore the intensity relationship among neighboring sampling points of a pixel, Wang et al. [16] proposed the Local Intensity Order Pattern (LIOP) for interest region description. Although both proposed for interest region description, the advantage of LIOP over CS-LBP is that it not only compares intensities between center-symmetric sampling points, but also compares intensities among nearby sampling points. Due to this intensity comparing strategy, LIOP is more discriminative than CS-LBP. Moreover, LIOP only uses 4 neighboring points instead of 8 neighboring points while achieving a better performance.

Given 4 neighboring points x_0, x_1, x_2, x_3 of a pixel x, their intensities are denoted by $I(x_0), I(x_1), I(x_2), I(x_3)$. As there are 24 possible permutations for 4 intensities, each permutation can be defined as a local intensity order pattern. A local intensity order pattern can be further represented by a 24-dimensional vector, with one element being 1 and the others being 0. Therefore, by sorting intensities of the 4 neighboring points of x, we can first obtain a permutation and then have its corresponding 24-dimensional vector as the local intensity order pattern of x. Please see Sect. 3.3 for more details about how to use it to construct a robust and distinctive descriptor for interest region matching.

References

1. Ahonen, T., Hadid, A., Pietikainen, M.: Face description with local binary patterns: Application to face recognition. IEEE Trans. Pattern Anal. Mach. Intell. **28**(12), 2037–2041 (2006)
2. Bay, H., Ess, A., Tuytelaars, T., Gool, L.V.: SURF: speeded up robust features. Comput. Vis. Image Underst. **110**(3), 346–359 (2008)
3. Bay, H., Tuytelaars, T., Gool, L.V.: SURF: Speeded up robust features. In: European Conference on Computer Vision, pp. 404–417 (2006)
4. Dalal, N., Triggs, B.: Histograms of oriented gradients for human detection. In: IEEE Conference on Computer Vision and Pattern Recognition, pp. 886–893 (2005)
5. Friedman, J., Hastie, T., Tibshirani, R.: Additive logistic regression: a statistical view of boosting. Ann. Stat. **28**(2), 337–407 (2000)
6. Heikkila, M., Pietikainen, M., Schmid, C.: Description of interest regions with center-symmetric local binary patterns. In: 5th Indian Conference on Computer Vision, Graphics and Image Processing, pp. 58–69 (2006)
7. Liao, S., Zhao, G., Kellokumpu, V., Pietikainen, M., Li, S.: Modeling pixel process with scale invariant local patterns for background subtraction in complex scenes. In: IEEE Conference on Computer Vision and Pattern Recognition, pp. 1301–1306 (2010)
8. Liao, S., Zhu, X., Lei, Z., Zhang, L., Li, S.: Learning multi-scale block local binary patterns for face recognition. In: International Conference on Biometrics, pp. 828–837 (2007)
9. Lowe, D.: Distinctive image features from scale-invariant keypoints. Int. J. Comput. Vis. **60**(2), 91–110 (2004)
10. Neubeck, A., Van Gool, L.: Efficient non-maximum suppression. Int. Conf. Pattern Recogn. **3**, 850–855 (2006)
11. Ojala, T., Pietikainen, M., Harwood, D.: A comparative study of texture measures with classification based on feature distributions. Pattern Recogn. **29**, 51–59 (1996)
12. Ojala, T., Pietikainen, M., Maenpaa, T.: Multiresolution gray-scale and rotation invariant texture classification with local binary patterns. IEEE Trans. Pattern Anal. Mach. Intell. **24**(7), 971–987 (2002)
13. Pietikainen, M., Hadid, A., Zhao, G., Ahonen, T.: Computer Vision Using Local Binary Patterns. Springer (2011)
14. Pietikainen, M., Ojala, T., Xu, Z.: Rotation-invariant texture classification using feature distributions. Pattern Recogn. **33**, 43–52 (2000)
15. Tan, X., Triggs, B.: Enhanced local texture feature sets for face recognition under difficult lighting conditions. IEEE Trans. Image Process. **19**(6), 1635–1650 (2010)

16. Wang, Z., Fan, B., Wu, F.: Local intensity order pattern for feature description. In: International Conference on Computer Vision, pp. 603–610 (2011)
17. Zhang, W., Shan, S., Gao, W., Chen, X., Zhang, H.: Local gabor binary pattern histogram sequence (LGBPHS): A novel non-statistical model for face representation and recognition. In: International Conference on Computer Vision, pp. 786–791 (2005)

Chapter 3
Intensity Order-Based Local Descriptors

Abstract In this chapter, we discuss the local descriptors which exploit intensity order information. The good property of intensity order is that it is invariant to monotonic brightness change, which has been well studied in recent years, leading to the state-of-the-art descriptors for image matching. It has been used in both feature construction and feature pooling. We first discuss the most straightforward method using intensity order information in a local image patch, which creates a 2D histogram of intensity order and location for feature description. Next, we elaborate a new feature description framework by intensity order-based pooling. Then, a local intensity order pattern (LIOP) and how it is used in this framework are introduced. Finally, we demonstrate how we can design a binary descriptor by using the ordinal information in the local image patch.

Keywords Pooling by intensity order · Rotation invariant descriptors · LIOP · MROGH · Order based descriptors

3.1 Ordinal and Spatial Intensity Distribution Descriptor (OSID)

To encode the intensity order information into a descriptor, maybe the most straightforward method is to compute a histogram of intensity order for different subregions in a local image patch. This is the basic idea of Ordinal and Spatial Intensity Distribution (OSID) descriptor [14]. Briefly speaking, it captures both the ordinal and spatial distribution of pixels in a local image patch and uses their joint distribution as the feature descriptor.

More specifically, given a local image patch around a keypoint, it is first smoothed with a Gaussian filter (5×5 size and $\sigma = 1$) to remove noise since relative ordering of the pixel intensities is sensitive to noise. Then, all pixels in the local patch are sorted according to their intensities, assigning an order number to each pixel (ordinal labeling). Meanwhile, the local patch is divided into m pies. Finally, the OSID descriptor is constructed by computing a histogram of orders in each pie area and concatenating them together. Suppose there are n bins in the histogram of orders, a pixel with order number x in the ith pie area is contributed to the $\lceil \frac{x}{N} n \rceil$ bin in

© Springer-Verlag Berlin Heidelberg 2015
B. Fan et al., *Local Image Descriptor: Modern Approaches*,
SpringerBriefs in Computer Science, DOI 10.1007/978-3-662-49173-7_3

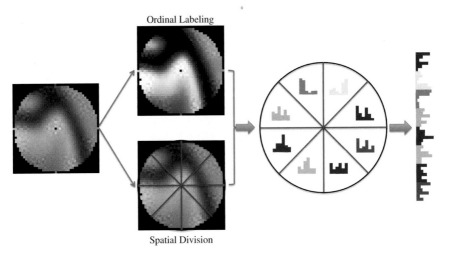

Fig. 3.1 The pipeline of computing OSID descriptor

the ith histogram, where N is the number of pixels in the patch. The concatenated descriptor is normalized with the number of pixels (N) to eliminate its effect on the descriptor. The whole procedure of computing OSID descriptor is illustrated in Fig. 3.1. A typical value of m and n is 16 and 8, respectively.

3.2 Intensity Order-Based Pooling for Feature Description

In order to improve the discriminative ability of local descriptors, it is important to divide the local image patch into several subregions, then compute a feature representation for each of them, and finally concatenate these representations together. We call this procedure of dividing local image patch into several parts and concatenating the computed representations as pooling. Traditional method for this purpose is geometrical spatial pooling which relies on a geometric layout. For example, the grid layout used in SIFT [12], SURF [2] and CS-LBP [8], and the concentric circles layout used in spin image [10]. In this section, we will first give an analysis on the geometric-based spatial pooling. After that, we elaborate a recently proposed intensity order-based pooling, which can be taken as a new framework for feature description. Finally, we show how it can be used to pool low-level image features such as gradient and CS-LBP to obtain the state-of-the-art feature descriptors [6], i.e., MROGH (Multisupport Region Order-based Gradient Histogram) and MRRID (Multisupport Region Rotation and Intensity monotonic invariant Descriptor).

3.2.1 An Analysis of the Geometric-Based Spatial Pooling

For geometric-based spatial pooling, it can be roughly classified into two categories according to whether it requires an additional reference orientation or not in order to be rotation invariant. The first category relies on a reference orientation to align the local image patch, and it divides the patch into grid, either in the Cartesian coordinate system or in the polar coordinate system. Many famous local descriptors belong to this category, for example, SIFT [12] and SURF [2] use the grid layout in the Cartesian coordinate system, while DAISY [15, 18] uses the grid layout in the polar coordinate system. On the contrary, the second category achieves rotation invariance without referring to an estimated orientation of the local image patch. As a result, only the ring-shaped spatial pooling area (concentric circles layout) is possible. The spin image and RIFT [10] belong to this category. The advantage of the grid layout over the concentric circles layout is that more information about the spatial distribution of low-level features can be captured, thus, the descriptors belonging to the first category are usually more discriminative. However, the disadvantage of the grid layout is that it relies on an additional reference orientation, whose estimation is an error-prone procedure. The error existed in orientation estimation will in turn degrade the performance of the corresponding local descriptor.

To experimentally show that orientation estimation error will make many true corresponding points unmatchable by their descriptors, 40 image pairs with rotation transformation (some of them also involve scale changes) are collected from the Internet.[1] Each of them is related by a homography that is supplied along with the image pair. They are captured from five types of scenes with different textures and structures.

For each image pair, SIFT descriptors were extracted on the detected SIFT keypoints and were matched by the nearest neighbor of the distances of their descriptors. For a pair of corresponding points (x, y, θ) and (x', y', θ') which are determined according to the groundtruth homography, the orientation estimation error is computed by:

$$\varepsilon = \theta' - f(\theta; H) \tag{3.1}$$

where $f(\theta; H)$ is the groundtruth orientation of θ in the second image by transforming the first image to the second image according to the homography H between the two images. Figure 3.2 presents some statistical results. Figure 3.2a is the histogram of orientation estimation errors among all corresponding points. Note that a similar histogram was also obtained by Winder and Brown [17] by applying random synthetic affine warps. Figure 3.2b shows the histogram of orientation estimation errors among those corresponding points that were also matched by their SIFT descriptors. It indicates that for SIFT descriptor, orientation estimation error of no more than

---

[1]http://lear.inrialpes.fr/people/mikolajczyk/.

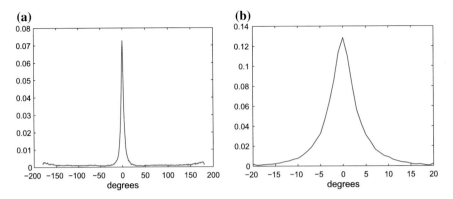

Fig. 3.2 Distributions of the orientation estimation errors between corresponding points. **a** The distribution among all the corresponding points, only 63.77 % of the corresponding points have errors in the range of $[-20°, 20°]$. **b** The distribution among those corresponding points that were also matched by their SIFT descriptors. ©[2012] IEEE. Reprinted, with permission, from Fan et al. [6]

$20°$ is required in order to match corresponding points correctly. However, it can be clearly seen from Fig. 3.2a that many corresponding points have errors larger than $20°$. In this experiment, only 63.77 % of the corresponding points have orientation estimation errors in the range of $[-20°, 20°]$. Those corresponding points with large orientation estimation errors ($\geq 20°$) may not be correctly matched by comparing their descriptors. In other words, 36.23 % of the corresponding points were incorrectly matched mainly due to their large orientation estimation errors. Therefore, orientation estimation has a significant impact on the discriminative power of the constructed descriptor.

In order to give more insight into the influence of the estimated orientation on the matching performance of local descriptor, some image matching experiments were conducted. The experimental images are shown in Fig. 3.3a–f. For each image pair, there exists a global rotation between the two images. Specifically, $0°$ for image pairs in Fig. 3.3d–f, and a certain degree for image pairs in Fig. 3.3a–c. Two local descriptors (SIFT and DAISY) with two different orientation assignment methods were used for image matching:

(1) The orientation is assigned by the groundtruth orientation, and the constructed local descriptors are denoted as **Ori-SIFT** and **Ori-DAISY**.
(2) The orientation is assigned with the method used in SIFT [12], and the constructed local descriptors are denoted as **SIFT** and **DAISY**.

Additionally, two subsets from the Patch Dataset [3] are tested. In each subset, there are 20,000 matching patches and nonmatching patches. Since there exists no or small orientation between matching patches, **Ori-SIFT (Ori-DAISY)** is obtained by constructing descriptor directly on the patch, while **SIFT (DAISY)** is obtained by first rotating the patch randomly and then constructing the descriptor according to the orientation estimated by [12].

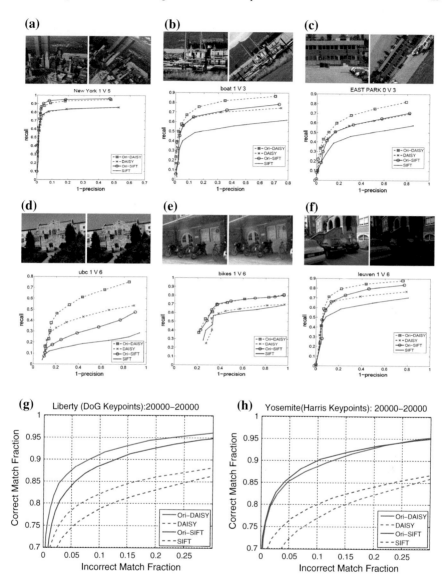

Fig. 3.3 Image matching results of SIFT and DAISY when using the estimated orientation and the groundtruth orientation (Ori-SIFT, Ori-DAISY). Results on image pairs of **a** 45° rotation, **b** 40° rotation + 0.75 scale changes, **c** 50° rotation + 0.6 scale changes, **d** JPEG compression, **e** image blur, **f** illumination change, **g** is the result on the Brown's local image patch dataset [3] from DoG keypoints, and **h** is the result on local image patches from scale invariant Harris Keypoints. ©[2012] IEEE. Reprinted, with permission, from Fan et al. [6]

By comparing the performance of **Ori-SIFT/Ori-DAISY** with **SIFT/DAISY**, it is clear to understand the influence of the orientation estimation on constructing local descriptor for image matching. Experimental results are shown below

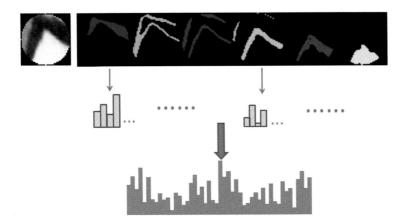

Fig. 3.4 The intensity order-based framework for feature description. ©[2012] IEEE. Reprinted, with permission, from Fan et al. [6]

the tested image pairs in Fig. 3.3a–f. Figure 3.3g, h show results on the Patch Dataset. It can be seen from Fig. 3.3 that **Ori-SIFT/Ori-DAISY** significantly outperforms **SIFT/DAISY**. Since the only difference between **Ori-SIFT/Ori-DAISY** and **SIFT/DAISY** is the orientation assignment method, it is obvious that a more accurate orientation estimation will largely improve the performance of the local descriptor. The currently used orientation estimation method based on the histogramming technique is still an error-prone procedure and will adversely affect the performance of the local descriptor. Some other work [2, 4] also noticed that orientation estimation will degrade the performance if we do not need this kind of invariance.

3.2.2 Intensity Order-Based Patch Division

The drawbacks in geometric-based spatial pooling motivate a new framework for feature description [6] as shown in Fig. 3.4, at the core of which is an intensity order-based patch division strategy. It first partitions the local image patch into several parts according to the intensity orders of its pixels (first row in Fig. 3.4), then a feature representation is obtained for each part (second row in Fig. 3.4) as in case of geometric-based spatial pooling, and finally all the feature representations of all the parts are concatenated together as the feature descriptor (third row in Fig. 3.4).

Suppose the local image patch around a keypoint is denoted by $\Omega = \{X_1, X_2, \ldots, X_n\}$, and $I(X)$ denotes the intensity of pixel X. First, the intensities of all pixels in Ω are sorted in a non-descending order to obtain an ordered set:

$$O(\Omega) = \{I(\hat{X}_i) : I(\hat{X}_1) \leq I(\hat{X}_2) \leq \cdots \leq I(\hat{X}_n), \hat{X}_i \in \Omega, i \in [1, n]\} \quad (3.2)$$

To uniformly divide Ω into m parts, $(m + 1)$ thresholds $\{t_0, t_1, \ldots, t_m\}$ are taken as:

$$t_0 = I(\hat{X}_1)$$
$$t_k = I(\hat{X}_{b_k}), k = 1, 2, \ldots, m - 1 \tag{3.3}$$
$$t_m = I(\hat{X}_n)$$

where

$$b_k = \lfloor k/m \times n \rfloor \tag{3.4}$$

Based on these thresholds, the n pixels in the local patch are partitioned into m parts,

$$R_i = \{X_j \in \Omega : t_{i-1} \leq I(X_j) \leq t_i\}, \quad i = 1, 2, \ldots, m \tag{3.5}$$

In the first row of Fig. 3.4, it gives an illustration of such an intensity order-based patch division. Each partitioned part is called a subregion and marked with a specific color. It is worth noting that this method does not rotate the patch according to a local consistent orientation to achieve rotational invariance. The intensity order-based patch division is inherently invariant to monotonic intensity changes and image rotation. Meanwhile, since it captures more information than the ring-shaped patch division, it is much more distinctive.

Under this framework, it is apparent that different descriptors can be obtained by using different low-level features. Currently, the top performance descriptors in the widely used benchmark (Oxford's VGG Dataset [13]) are from this kind. Among these descriptors, some of them are simply using existed low-level features such as those used in SIFT and CS-LBP, resulting in MROGH and MRRID [6]. Others are based on the special intensity order-based low-level feature which we will introduce in the next section. As an example of using the intensity order-based pooling framework for feature description, in the next part, we briefly introduce how to construct MROGH and MRRID.

3.2.3 Construction of MROGH and MRRID Descriptors

Since the motivation of using intensity order-based pooling is to achieve rotation invariance without estimating a reference orientation, the used low-level feature should also be computed in an inherently rotation invariant way. For this purpose, a locally rotation invariant coordinate system is constructed for each pixel in the local image patch. As shown in Fig. 3.5, suppose P is a keypoint and X_i is one pixel in its support region (a local image patch around the keypoint used for constructing descriptor). Then a local xy coordinate system can be established for each pixel X_i in the local image patch by setting $\overrightarrow{PX_i}$ as the positive y-axis.

Under this local coordinate system, similar to SIFT [12] and DAISY [15], we can compute an eighth-dimensional vector for each pixel in the local image patch by linearly assigning the gradient orientation to its neighboring two bins weighted by the gradient magnitude. Denoting this vector as $f_G(X_i)$, we can obtain

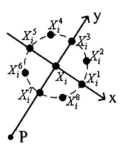

Fig. 3.5 The locally rotation invariant coordinate system, which is used for calculating low-level feature of a pixel X_i in the local image patch for feature description. P is the keypoint. ©[2012] IEEE. Reprinted, with permission, from Fan et al. [6]

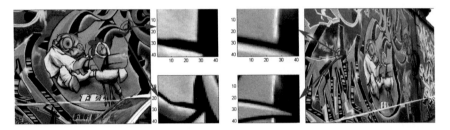

Fig. 3.6 Motivation of using multiple support regions. Two non-corresponding keypoints may have similar appearances in a certain local region, but it is less possible that they have similar appearances in several local regions of different sizes

the feature descriptor as $F_{\text{OGH}} = [\sum_{X_i \in R_1} f_G(X_i), \ldots, \sum_{X_i \in R_m} f_G(X_i)] \in \mathfrak{R}^{8m}$, which is called order-based gradient histogram (OGH). A similar normalization as SIFT is applied to OGH to deal with illumination change. Similarly, by computing the CS-LBP [8] in this coordinate system, we can get a 16-dimensional vector $f_I(X_i)$ for X_i. The generated feature descriptor is computed by $F_{\text{RID}} = [\sum_{X_i \in R_1} f_I(X_i), \ldots, \sum_{X_i \in R_m} f_I(X_i)] \in \mathfrak{R}^{16m}$, followed by a normalization to unit length. This kind of descriptor is called rotation and intensity monotonic invariant descriptor (RID). m is usually set to be six.

To further improve the discriminative power of the descriptor, using multiple support regions is an effective strategy. As depicted in Fig. 3.6, using only one single support region is not enough to distinguish some keypoints. However, it is much easier if using multiple support regions because it is less possible for two non-corresponding keypoints to have similar local appearances in several local regions with different sizes. Based on this observation, OGH and RID can be constructed with multiple support regions, obtaining the MROGH and MRRID. Concretely, we use n gradually increased support regions (n is usually set to be 4), which are normalized to an uniform size e.g., 41×41). Then, a feature descriptor is computed for each of them. These descriptors are concatenated together and normalized to unit length to form the final descriptor.

3.3 Local Intensity Order Pattern for Feature Description

The low-level features play an important role in both distinctiveness and robustness of the constructed feature descriptors. Previous work [6–8] has shown the effectiveness of using LBP-like low-level features in feature description. However, since these methods only compare the intensities of central symmetric sampling points, they do not effectively capture the intensity relationships among all the sampling points and suffers a relatively low discriminative ability.

LIOP (Local Intensity Order Pattern) is proposed to overcome this problem [16]. It effectively explores the local ordinal information by using the intensity order among all the sampling points around a pixel.

Before the formal definition of LIOP, some basic mappings are introduced. Let Π^N be the set of all possible permutations of integers $\{1, 2, \ldots, N\}$, the mapping $\gamma : \Re^N \longrightarrow \Pi^N$ is defined to map an N-dimensional vector $Y \in \Re^N$ to a permutation $\pi = \gamma(Y) \in \Pi^N$ based on the orders of the N elements of Y, i.e., $y_1, y_2, \ldots, y_N$. More specifically, the mapping γ sorts the N elements of Y into a non-descending order, $y_{i_1} \leq y_{i_2} \leq \cdots \leq y_{i_N}$, and uses the subscript list $(i_1, i_2, \ldots, i_N)$ as the permutation. To avoid ambiguity, it defines $y_s \leq y_t$ if and only if (i) $y_s < y_t$, or (ii) $y_s = y_t$ and $s < t$.

Since there are $N!$ permutations for N values, Π^N has a cardinality of $N!$. Therefore, each $\pi \in \Pi^N$ can be uniquely represented by an integer ranging from 1 to $N!$. Each of these integers is predefined to be corresponded to a specific permutation. Such correspondences are stored in an index table as shown in the middle of Fig. 3.7 in case of $N = 4$. This mapping is denoted as $\phi : \Pi^N \longrightarrow \{1, 2, \ldots, N!\}$.

With the above defined mappings, the LIOP code of a pixel X_i in a local patch is an integer defined as:

$$LIOP(X_i) = \phi(\gamma(Y(X_i))) \tag{3.6}$$

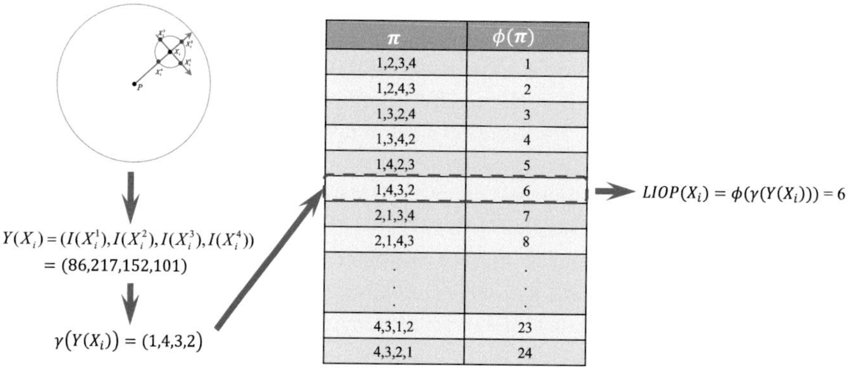

π	$\phi(\pi)$
1,2,3,4	1
1,2,4,3	2
1,3,2,4	3
1,3,4,2	4
1,4,2,3	5
1,4,3,2	6
2,1,3,4	7
2,1,4,3	8
.	.
.	.
4,3,1,2	23
4,3,2,1	24

$Y(X_i) = (I(X_i^1), I(X_i^2), I(X_i^3), I(X_i^4))$
$= (86, 217, 152, 101)$

$\gamma(Y(X_i)) = (1, 4, 3, 2)$

$LIOP(X_i) = \phi(\gamma(Y(X_i))) = 6$

Fig. 3.7 An illustration of computing LIOP code for a pixel X_i in the local image patch centered at P when 4 neighboring sample points are used. P is the keypoint. ©[2011] IEEE. Reprinted, with permission, from Wang et al. [16]

where $Y(X_i) = (I(X_i^1), I(X_i^2), \ldots, I(X_i^N)) \in \Re^N$ is the vector constituted by the intensities of the N regularly sampled neighboring points of X_i. Note that these neighboring points are sampled in the locally rotation invariant coordinate system depicted in Fig. 3.5 to ensure rotation invariance. According to the experiments in [16], N is set as 4.

3.3.1 Construction of the LIOP Descriptor

Similar to construction of the MROGH/MRRID descriptors, LIOP is constructed by collecting all the LIOP codes in each intensity order-based partition separately. For each pixel X_i in the local image patch, its LIOP code is first converted into an $N!$ dimensional vector $b(X_i) \in \{0, 1\}^{N!}$, which has only one element to be 1 and others are 0. In $b(X_i)$, the element corresponding to $\text{LIOP}(X_i)$ is set to be 1. Therefore, the LIOP descriptor is computed by $F_{\text{LIOP}} = [\sum_{X_i \in R_1} b(X_i), \ldots, \sum_{X_i \in R_m} b(X_i)] \in \Re^{mN!}$, followed by a normalization to unit length. With a typical parameter setting of $m = 6$ and $N = 4$, the LIOP descriptor has a dimension of 144. Although LIOP can be used with the strategy of multiple support regions introduced in the last section, it is mostly used with only one single support region. The reason is that using multiple support regions will significantly increase the dimensionality of the descriptor as the basic LIOP descriptor is 144 dimensional. Moreover, even with one single support region, LIOP performs rather well in most cases, only a little inferior to MROGH and MRRID.

3.4 Intensity Order-Based Binary Descriptor

As binary descriptors[2] are becoming widely used in computer vision due to their high matching efficiency and low memory requirements, here we show how intensity order can be used in designing a rotation invariant binary descriptor, called Ordinal and Spatial information of Regional Invariants (OSRI) [19]. This binary descriptor is largely inspired by the intensity order-based pooling, mainly for its ability to achieve rotation invariance without resorting to a reference orientation while maintaining high distinctiveness.

Different from the widely used strategy of comparing pixel intensities in constructing binary descriptors (BRIEF [4], BRISK [11], FREAK [1], etc.), it resorts to compare the regional invariants which are computed from the subregions obtained on the basis of intensity orders and gradient orientation orders of pixels in the local image patch. Basically, computing an OSRI descriptor involves three steps: (1) Dividing the local image patch into subregions according to the orders of intensities and gradient orientations of pixels in the patch; (2) Computing some regional invariants for each

---

[2]We will give a detailed introduction to them in Chap. 4.

subregion; (3) Comparing some predefined regional invariants between some pre-defined pairs of subregions to obtain the binary descriptor. The predefined regional invariants as well as the predefined pairs of subregions are automatically determined by a machine learning algorithm. In the following, we will first describe in details how to generate a set of candidate subregions based on intensity orders and gradient orientation orders. Then, we elaborate the regional invariants computed from these subregions. Based on their properties, they are used to generate pairwise compar-isons of regional invariants. Finally, we give an algorithm to select a small set of such pairwise comparisons from all the possible ones to define the OSRI descriptor.

3.4.1 Subregions Generation

The first step of constructing OSRI is to divide the local image patch into informative subregions. These subregions should not only be rotation invariant without resorting to a reference orientation, but also contain information of appearance, shape and spatial geometry as rich as possible. Inspired by the good properties of the intensity order-based patch division introduced in Sect. 3.2, OSRI improves it in two aspects: (1) Besides the intensity order-based patch division, it also uses the gradient orien-tation orders to divide the patch into subregions. The two complementary properties make the resulted subregions contain more appearance, shape, and spatial character-istics. (2) The circular-shift operation is used to obtain more subregions in a given local patch for feature description.

Suppose a local image patch is denoted by $R = \{X_1, X_2, \ldots, X_n\}$. We further denote $I(X_i)$ as the intensity of pixel X_i, and $\theta(X_i) \in [0, 2\pi]$ as its gradient orien-tation. Note that to ensure inherently rotation invariance, the gradient is computed in the locally coordinate system as depicted in Fig. 3.5. The purpose of patch division is to divide R into k_u and k_v subregions according to the intensity orders and the gra-dient direction orders of all pixels respectively. This procedure is repeated K times by the circular-shift operation. Therefore, it will results in $K \times (k_u + k_v)$ subregions.

More specifically, all pixels in R are first sorted by their intensities in a non-descending order, and a set of sorted pixels is obtained as:

$$R^I = \{X_{f_1}, X_{f_2}, \ldots, X_{f_n} : I(X_{f_1}) \leq I(X_{f_2}) \leq \cdots \leq I(X_{f_n})\} \quad (3.7)$$

where $f_1, f_2, \ldots, f_n$ is a permutation of $1, 2, \ldots, n$. By equally and sequentially dividing R^I into k_u parts, we can obtain k_u subregions accordingly. Therefore, by circular-shifting the elements in R^I K times, we can obtain K such subregions, obtaining a total number of $K \times k_u$ subregions. The footprint of the circular-shift operation is set to $p = \lceil \frac{1}{K} \frac{n}{k_u} \rceil$, thus, after K operations, the resulted subregions are identical. Mathematically, for the s-th circular-shift operation, the shifted set of the sorted pixels is:

$$R^I(s) = \{X_{h(f_1,s)}, X_{h(f_2,s)}, \ldots, X_{h(f_n,s)}\} \quad (3.8)$$

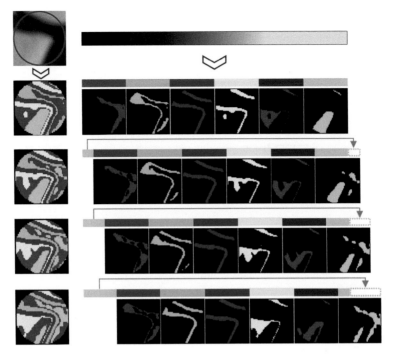

Fig. 3.8 An illustration of intensity order-based patch division. It can be seen that the circular-shift operator is used to group all pixels in the local patch in different ways. ©[2014] IEEE. Reprinted, with permission, from Xu et al. [19]

where $h(f_i, s) = f_{(i+p(s-1))\%n}$ is the original position of the ith element in the shifted set. Figure 3.8 provides an illustration of this patch division method, where four circular-shift operations are used. For each shifted set of the sorted pixels, it is divided into six subregions marked with different colors.

Similarly, another set of sorted pixels can be obtained by sorting pixels in R according to their gradient orientations:

$$R^G = \{X_{g_1}, X_{g_2}, \ldots, X_{g_n} : \theta(X_{g_1}) \leq \theta(X_{g_2}) \leq \cdots \leq \theta(X_{g_n})\} \quad (3.9)$$

where $g_1, g_2, \ldots, g_n$ is a permutation of $1, 2, \ldots, n$. By equally and sequentially dividing the patch into k_v subregions, and with the same circular-shift operation, we can obtain $K \times k_v$ subregions.

According to the above procedure, we can obtain a total number of $N = K \times (k_u + k_v)$ subregions, denoted as $\{sR_1, sR_2, \ldots, sR_N\}$.

3.4.2 Regional Invariants and Pairwise Comparisons

After subregion division, the next step is to compute some measures and build pairwise comparisons among them to produce binary bits. To get a robust and discriminative binary descriptor in final, the computed measures should be robust to geometric and photometric changes of the local image patch, as well as capture a rich description of the local cues (appearance, shape and spatial geometry) in the meantime. For these purposes, 11 statistical invariants[3] computed from a subregion are used, which will be described in details in the following paragraphs. In general, they are grouped into three categories as they capture different properties of the subregion: moment invariants (algebraic ones and geometric ones), spatial distribution of the pixels in the subregion, and the geometric centroid of the subregion. Note that all these measures are rotation invariant. Meanwhile, except for the algebraic moment invariant computed from the gradient orientations, all the remaining 10 measures are invariant to monotonic intensity change too. This the reason why they are call invariants.

(a) *Moment invariants* Two kinds of moment invariants are used, namely the algebraic moment invariants and the geometric moment invariants. The algebraic moments are the intensity variance and the gradient magnitude variance. For the geometric moments, the Hu set of invariant moments [9] are used, which are invariant to translation, scale, and rotation. They are computed as follows:

$$\psi_1 = \eta_{20} + \eta_{02} \tag{3.10}$$

$$\psi_2 = (\eta_{20} - \eta_{02})^2 + 4\eta_{11}^2 \tag{3.11}$$

$$\psi_3 = (\eta_{30} - 3\eta_{12})^2 + (3\eta_{21} - \eta_{03})^2 \tag{3.12}$$

$$\psi_4 = (\eta_{30} + \eta_{12})^2 + (\eta_{21} + \eta_{03})^2 \tag{3.13}$$

$$\psi_5 = (\eta_{30} - 3\eta_{12})(\eta_{30} + \eta_{12})((\eta_{30} + \eta_{12})^2 - 3(\eta_{21} + \eta_{03})^2)$$
$$+ (3\eta_{21} - \eta_{03})(\eta_{21} + \eta_{03})(3(\eta_{30} + \eta_{12})^2 - (\eta_{21} + \eta_{03})^2) \tag{3.14}$$

$$\psi_6 = (\eta_{20} - \eta_{02})((\eta_{30} + \eta_{12})^2 - (\eta_{21} + \eta_{03})^2) + 4\eta_{11}(\eta_{30} + \eta_{12})(\eta_{21} + \eta_{03}) \tag{3.15}$$

$$\psi_7 = (3\eta_{21} - \eta_{03})(\eta_{30} + \eta_{12})((\eta_{30} + \eta_{12})^2 - 3(\eta_{21} + \eta_{03})^2)$$
$$- (\eta_{30} - 3\eta_{12})(\eta_{21} + \eta_{03})(3(\eta_{30} + \eta_{12})^2 - (\eta_{21} + \eta_{03})^2) \tag{3.16}$$

---

[3]The term 'invariants' mean that they are invariant to some certain kinds of geometric/photometric transformations.

where η_{pq} is defined as

$$n_{pq} = \frac{u_{pq}}{u_{00}^{\gamma}}, \gamma = \frac{p+q}{2} + 1 \tag{3.17}$$

and

$$u_{pq} = \iint\limits_{sR} (x - \bar{x})^p (y - \bar{y})^q I(x, y) d(x - \bar{x}) d(y - \bar{y}) \tag{3.18}$$

$$\bar{x} = \frac{m_{10}}{m_{00}}, \bar{y} = \frac{m_{01}}{m_{00}}, \tag{3.19}$$

$$m_{pq} = \iint\limits_{sR} x^p y^q I(x, y) dx dy, \quad p, q = 0, 1, \ldots, \tag{3.20}$$

In the above equations, sR is a subregion and $I(x, y)$ is the intensity of pixel in (x, y).

By comparing any specific kind of these moment invariants for any two subregions, we can get a candidate bit. Therefore, there are totally $9C_N^2$ such pairwise comparisons where N is the number of subregions.

(b) *Spatial distribution of pixels* To capture the spatial distribution of the pixels in each subregion, the local patch is first divided into m concentric rings of equal space. Then, for each subregion sR_i, we compute a histogram about how its pixels scatter in these m rings. Since the areas of different rings are different, it is important to normalize this factor in the corresponding bin of the histogram. As a result, we can obtain N histograms with m bins, which are computed as following:

$$\Phi_{ij} = \frac{1}{2j - 1} \left| \{(x, y) : (x, y) \in sR_i \text{ and } (x, y) \in \mathbb{O}_j\} \right|, i = 1, \ldots, N, j = 1, \ldots, m \tag{3.21}$$

where (x, y) is a pixel in the patch, $|\cdot|$ is the cardinality of a set, $\mathbb{O}_j$ denotes the jth concentric ring.

By pairwise comparing Φ_{ij}, we can obtain C_{mN}^2 comparisons.

(c) *Geometric centroid* For two matching keypoints, the spatial geometric relationship of their subregions should be identical; on the contrary, it should be dissimilar for a pair of nonmatching keypoints. The angles between the vectors connecting the keypoint and geometric centroids of its subregions can be used to encode this spatial geometric information. For a subregion sR_i, its geometric centroid can be computed as:

$$C_i = \left(\frac{m_{10}}{m_{00}}, \frac{m_{01}}{m_{00}} \right) \tag{3.22}$$

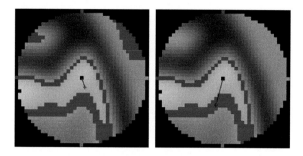

Fig. 3.9 *Left* The geometric centroid computed from an original subregion. *Right* The geometric centroid computed from its maximal connected component. Using the maximal connected component is less influenced by the approximately central symmetric distribution of pixels in the subregion

where

$$m_{pq} = \sum_{(x,y)\in sR_i} x^p y^q. \tag{3.23}$$

Assuming that P is the keypoint, let the direction of $\overrightarrow{PC_1}$ connecting P and C_1 be $0°$, $\theta_{\overrightarrow{PC_i}} \in [0, 2\pi)$, $i = 2, \ldots, N$, is taken as the angle between $\overrightarrow{PC_i}$ and $\overrightarrow{PC_1}$ anticlockwise. The authors of OSRI have noted that the geometric centroid of the original partitioned subregion is unstable as it is approximately central symmetric with respect to P in most cases [19]. To alleviate this problem, they proposed to extract the maximal connected component in a subregion, and use its geometric centroid C_i' to compute $\theta_{\overrightarrow{PC_i'}}$ instead of $\theta_{\overrightarrow{PC_i}}$. This is illustrated in Fig. 3.9

In total, there are N such directions. Therefore, C_N^2 pairwise comparisons are generated.

3.4.3 Learning Good Binary Descriptor

Based on the above mentioned 11 invariants and $N = K \times (k_u + k_v)$ subregions, a total number of $(9C_N^2 + C_{mN}^2 + C_N^2)$ pairwise comparisons can be obtained. With a typical parameter setting of $K = 4, k_u = 6, k_v = 6, m = 3$, there are 21,576 available bits. Therefore, a candidate set of 21,576 bits is ready for learning a good binary descriptor. Since there are many redundant bits that are not effective to describe the local patch, it uses an unsupervised learning algorithm to select a small set of less correlated bits to form the OSRI binary descriptor. More specifically, it first computes a long binary string of length 21,576 for each keypoint detected in the images of the PASCAL VOC 2007 dataset [5]. Then, it computes the mean values of these bits respectively across all the keypoints, and sorts them in an increasing order of $|0.5 - v|$, where v denotes the mean value. A smaller value of $|0.5 - v|$ means a higher variance of the bit, implying more information can be contained. Finally, it gradually selects bits one by one from the sorted set by checking the correlation between the examined one and the selected bits. If there exists any bit in the selected set whose correlation to the examined bit is higher than a threshold, the examined bit is not selected. The selection process continues until the target number of bits has been selected or all the bits have been examined.

3.4.4 Using Multiple Support Regions

Similar to the MROGH and MRRID descriptors introduced in Sect. 3.2, OSRI can also use multiple support regions to encode more discriminative information. In this case, each support region is partitioned into $K \times (k_u + k_v)$ subregions by the method proposed in the previous section. Therefore, for R support regions, $L = R \times N$ subregions can be obtained. Accordingly, $(9C_L^2 + C_{mL}^2 + C_L^2)$ available bits are generated. The learning algorithm for the final binary descriptor is similar to the case of using single support region, which is elaborated in the last section.

3.4.5 Cascade Filtering for Speeding up Matching

A good property of OSRI is that it can be organized into four categories (moment invariants are split into algebraic ones and geometric ones) according to the type of regional invariants used to generate the corresponding bit. Let f be the d-dimensional OSRI descriptor, by organizing its d bits according to the type of used regional invariants and arranging them in an ascending order, it can be rewritten as $f = [f_1 f_2 f_3 f_4]$, where $\# f_1 < \# f_2 < \# f_3 < \# f_4$ and $\#$ means the number of bits. According to the experiments reported in [19], all these 4 parts have a comparable discriminative ability. For this reason, they can be fitted into a cascade structure to speedup descriptor matching, as shown in Fig. 3.10. In this way, it only needs to compare very few bits to filter out most nonmatches in the descriptor matching stage.

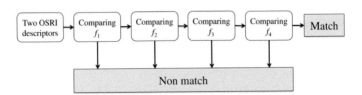

Fig. 3.10 A cascade structure can be constructed for matching OSRI descriptors by separating it into 4 parts (f_1, f_2, f_3, f_4) according to the type of used regional invariants

References

1. Alahi, A., Ortiz, R., Vandergheynst, P.: FREAK: Fast retina keypoint. In: IEEE Conference on Computer Vision and Pattern Recognition, pp. 10–517 (2012)
2. Bay, H., Ess, A., Tuytelaars, T., Gool, L.V.: SURF: speeded up robust features. Comput. Vis. Image Underst. **110**(3), 346–359 (2008)
3. Brown, M., Hua, G., Winder, S.: Discriminative learning of local image descriptors. IEEE Trans. Pattern Anal. Mach. Intell. **33**(1), 43–57 (2011)
4. Calonder, M., Lepetit, V., Ozuysal, M., Trzcinski, T., Strecha, C., Fua, P.: BRIEF: computing a local binary descriptor very fast. IEEE Trans. Pattern Anal. Mach. Intell. **33**(7), 1281–1298 (2012)
5. Everingham, M., Van Gool, L., Williams, C.K.I., Winn, J., Zisserman, A.: The Pascal Visual Object Classes (VOC) challenge. Int. J. Comput. Vision **88**(2), 303–338 (2010)
6. Fan, B., Wu, F., Hu, Z.: Rotationally invariant descriptors using intensity order pooling. IEEE Trans. Pattern Anal. Mach. Intell. **34**(10), 2031–2045 (2012)
7. Gupta, R., Patil, H., Mittal, A.: Robust order-based methods for feature description. In: IEEE Conference on Computer Vision and Pattern Recognition, pp. 334–341 (2010)
8. Heikkila, M., Pietikainen, M., Schmid, C.: Description of interest regions with local binary patterns. Pattern Recogn. **42**, 425–436 (2009)
9. Hu, M.K.: Visual pattern recognition by moment invariants. IRE Trans. Inf. Theory **8**(2), 179–187 (1962)
10. Lazebnik, S., Schmid, C., Ponce, J.: A sparse texture representation using local affine regions. IEEE Trans. Pattern Anal. Mach. Intell. **27**(8), 1265–1278 (2005)
11. Leutenegger, S., Chli, M., Siegwart, R.: BRISK: Binary robust invariant scalable keypoints. In: International Conference on Computer Vision, pp. 2548–2555 (2011)
12. Lowe, D.: Distinctive image features from scale-invariant keypoints. Int. J. Comput. Vision **60**(2), 91–110 (2004)
13. Mikolajczyk, K., Schmid, C.: A performance evaluation of local descriptors. IEEE Trans. Pattern Anal. Mach. Intell. **27**(10), 1615–1630 (2005)
14. Tang, F., Lim, S.H., Change, N.L., Tao, H.: A novel feature descriptor invariant to complex brightness changes. In: IEEE Conference on Computer Vision and Pattern Recognition, pp. 2631–2638 (2009)
15. Tola, E., Lepetit, V., Fua, P.: DAISY: An efficient dense descriptor applied to wide-baseline stereo. IEEE Trans. Pattern Anal. Mach. Intell. **32**(5), 815–830 (2010)
16. Wang, Z., Fan, B., Wu, F.: Local intensity order pattern for feature description.In: International Conference on Computer Vision, pp. 603–610 (2011)
17. Winder, S., Brown, M.: Learning local image descriptors. In: IEEE Conference on Computer Vision and Pattern Recognition, pp. 1–8 (2007)
18. Winder, S., Hua, G., Brown, M.: Picking the best DAISY. In: IEEE Conference on Computer Vision and Pattern Recognition, pp. 178–185 (2009)
19. Xu, X., Tian, L., Feng, J., Zhou, J.: OSRI: a rotationally invariant binary descriptor. IEEE Trans. Image Process. **23**(7), 2983–2995 (2014)

Chapter 4
Burgeoning Methods: Binary Descriptors

Abstract Binary descriptor requires much less storage than that of traditional descriptors, i.e., float vector descriptors. Meanwhile, the Hamming distance used for evaluating similarity between binary descriptors can be computed much faster than computing Euclidean distance between float vector descriptors. As a result, binary descriptor is becoming a popular solution to applications that require real-time processing or with limited memory resources. It has been a hot topic in the area of local image description in recent years and many binary descriptors have been proposed. In this chapter, we will introduce several representative methods.

Keywords Binary descriptors · Low memory footprint · Fast descriptor computation and matching · Real time image matching · Large scale image matching

4.1 BRIEF: Binary Robust Independent Elementary Features

The idea of using intensity test to extract local feature was first proposed more than 20 years ago by Local Binary Pattern (LBP) [20], which uses intensity tests between neighboring points and the central point to obtain the local pattern of the central point. However, LBP is always used along with the histogram technique. Therefore, the actual used feature for subsequent processing (e.g., face recognition, face detection, texture recognition) is a float-type vector. BRIEF [4] is the pioneer work that constructs a binary descriptor directly used for other applications, such as image matching and object recognition.

Given an image patch I of size $S \times S$, its BRIEF descriptor can be computed by:

$$B(I) = [t(I; p_1^{(1)}, p_1^{(2)}), t(I; p_2^{(1)}, p_2^{(2)}), \ldots, t(I; p_n^{(1)}, p_n^{(2)})] \in \{0, 1\}^n \quad (4.1)$$

where

$$t(I; p_i^{(1)}, p_i^{(2)}) = \begin{cases} 1, & I(p_i^{(1)}) \geq I(p_i^{(2)}) \\ 0, & I(p_i^{(1)}) < I(p_i^{(2)}) \end{cases} \quad (4.2)$$

© Springer-Verlag Berlin Heidelberg 2015
B. Fan et al., *Local Image Descriptor: Modern Approaches*,
SpringerBriefs in Computer Science, DOI 10.1007/978-3-662-49173-7_4

$t(I; p_i^{(1)}, p_i^{(2)})$ means an intensity difference test between a pair of positions ($p_i^{(1)}$ and $p_i^{(2)}$) in patch I, and $I(p_i)$ denotes the intensity value of pixel p_i in I. It can be seen that the position pairs play a core role in the construction of BRIEF descriptor. The original BRIEF was proposed to randomly select n pairs of positions according to the Gaussian distribution. More specifically, assuming the center of an image patch (with size $S \times S$) to be described is the origin of the used coordinate system, ($p_i^{(1)}, p_i^{(2)}, i = 1, \ldots, n$) are independently and identically distributed (i.i.d.) variables sampled from $N(0, \frac{S^2}{25})$. How to design a specific position pairs, not random ones, will be introduced in the later sections of this chapter.

Since intensity comparison is sensitive to noise, it is useful to adopt a smooth step before computing the BRIEF descriptor. Due to the simplicity and efficiency of box filter, a 7×7 box filter is found to be a good practise. Compared to the widely used Gaussian filter in the area of image processing, it is much faster to compute response of a box filter based on the integral image using only three additions, independent on the filter size. What is more, lots of studies have experimentally shown that there is no or little performance loss when using a box filter instead of a Gaussian filter.

To sum up, constructing a BRIEF descriptor for an input image patch contains the following steps:

(1) Smoothing the input image patch by a 7×7 box filter based on integral images.
(2) Conducting the intensity difference test based on the n given position pairs.
(3) Obtaining and outputting an n-dimensional binary descriptor according to the intensity test results.

Usually, n is set to be 256 as it comprises well between matching performance and efficiency. The performance will slightly be improved when n is increased from 256 to 512, but the memory footprint as well as the time of computing Hamming distance will also increase. Moreover, increasing n to more than 512 will not gain further improvement.

4.2   ORB: Oriented FAST and Rotated BRIEF

The biggest advantage of BRIEF lies in its efficiency. It could achieve moderate matching performance with only a very small amount of computations. However, BRIEF has its own intrinsic disadvantages, i.e., it cannot deal with scale and rotation changes. To alleviate these disadvantages, ORB [22] is proposed by incorporating a scale invariant FAST detector for keypoint detection and an intensity centroid-based method for keypoint orientation computation. Moreover, ORB proposed a simple but effective learning strategy for selecting salient and uncorrelated bits to form the descriptor from thousands of candidates.

4.2.1   Scale Invariant FAST Detector

FAST (Features from Accelerated Segment Test) [21] is an extremely efficient corner/feature detector. It uses a circle of 16 pixels to decide if the central pixel is corner or not. The classification is simply based on comparing intensities of these pixels to the central pixel. Specifically, if at least 12 continuous pixels are brighter or darker (at least by a predefined threshold t) than the central pixel, the central pixel is classified to be a corner. In fact, it is not necessary to test all the 16 pixels in cases of a non-corner pixel. Therefore, it is very fast to utilize FAST for feature detection.

One problem of FAST is that it does not produce a measure of cornerness as other methods, for instance, Harris corner detector [9]. Meanwhile, there are many detected corners located along edges, which are not stable for later description and matching. To remove these unstable corners, ORB proposed to use a Harris cornerness measure to rank the FAST corners and only keep the top N, which is the desired number of keypoints. This can be achieved by setting a low threshold t to first get more than N FAST features and then take the top N.

Another problem of FAST is that it does not have scale invariance. This problem is simply addressed using a scale pyramid of the image, and detecting the Harris filtered FAST corners at each level of the pyramid.

4.2.2   Orientation Computation by Intensity Centriod

Like most local descriptors, a local consistent orientation has to be computed for each feature so as to be rotation invariant. For efficiency, ORB uses the intensity centriod to compute this orientation. The intensity centriod is defined by:

$$C = \left(\frac{m_{10}}{m_{00}}, \frac{m_{01}}{m_{00}} \right) \tag{4.3}$$

where m_{pq} is the moment computed as:

$$m_{pq} = \sum_{x,y} x^p y^q I(x, y) \tag{4.4}$$

Thus, the direction from the central pixel (feature point) to C is defined as the orientation of this feature point. These moments are computed in a circular region of radius r around the feature point, and r is set to the patch size, i.e., the local region around the feature point for descriptor construction, whose typical value is 31×31.

It is worth to note that the ORB detector is very fast to compute for detecting feature points with scale and orientation information. This is due to the simplicity of the utilized strategies.

4.2.3 Learning Good Binary Features

With the detected scale and rotation of each feature point, ORB descriptor can be computed by first extracting a scale and rotation normalized local patch, and then computing BRIEF descriptor on the patch. However, as this orientation is computed based on the intensities of the described patch, the intensity relationship between the rotated pairs of positions used in BRIEF will move toward some fixed pattern. In this way, there are correlations among these position pairs that are used for computing the binary descriptor. Such correlation will reduce the discriminative ability of the descriptor. Therefore, randomly selecting 256 test pairs is not a good choice for ORB. One way to conquer this problem is to leverage on the training data to select informative and uncorrected bit features.

Given a local image patch in size of $m \times m$, and suppose the local window (i.e., the box filter used in BRIEF) used for intensity test is of size $r \times r$, there are $N = (m - r)^2$ such local windows. Each two of them can define an intensity test, so we have C_N^2 bit features. In the original implementation of ORB, m is set to 31, generating 228,150 binary tests. After removing tests that overlap, we finally have a set of 205,590 candidate bit features. Based on a training set, ORB selects at most 256 bits according to Algorithm 1.

Algorithm 1 Binary Feature Learning

Input:
    A set of candidate bit features: $\mathbb{F} = \{b_1, b_2, \ldots, b_k\}, k = 205, 590$; a training set of n local image patches; a threshold t to control the correlation between selected features.
Output:
    A set of bit features $\mathbb{B}$.
1: For each candidate bit feature, compute its value on all the training patches, obtaining an $n \times k$ matrix $A = [a_1, a_2, \ldots, a_k]$.
2: In each column of A, compute a distance between its mean value and 0.5.
3: Sort all columns in an increasing order of their distances, getting a permutation $s_1, s_2, \ldots, s_k$.
4: **for** $i = 1$ to k **do**
5:     Compute the correlation between a_{s_i} and each element in $\mathbb{B}$.
6:     **if** All the correlations are less than t **then**
7:         Add the s_ith feature into $\mathbb{B}$
8:     **end if**
9:     **if** The size of $\mathbb{B}$ achieves 256 **then**
10:        Terminate the learning procedure and output $\mathbb{B}$.
11:    **end if**
12: **end for**
13: **Output:** $\mathbb{B}$

From Algorithm 1, we can see that it defines the goodness of a bit feature as the distance between its mean value and 0.5. This is because that without any label information (either matching or not) about the training patches, a bit feature with large variance means that it generates different responses to different inputs, thus higher discriminative ability is expected. As the largest variance corresponds to a mean of 0.5, one can measure how good a bit feature is by computing the distance between its mean and 0.5. With the supervised label information, one can use more powerful measure to replace it and better performance can be expected. Fan et al. [5] have shown this point with another kind of bit features.

4.3 BRISK: Binary Robust and Invariant Scalable Keypoints

Both ORB and BRISK are proposed in ICCV 2011. Their motivations are similar, i.e., to alleviate the disadvantages of BRIEF. For this purpose, BRISK [14] also has its own feature detector and binary descriptor. Like ORB, its feature detector can detect keypoints with scale and orientation information too. As far as the binary descriptor is concerned, BRISK is also based on comparing intensities between two sampling patterns, but with a different sampling and feature selection strategy.

4.3.1 Keypoint Detection

To detect keypoint along with a scale information, it is necessary to construct a scale space pyramid as many works do [17, 22]. The scale space pyramid implemented in ORB is very fast to compute, but it divides scale space coarsely; on the contrary, the one implemented in SIFT is fine separated, but it is slow to compute. To compromise these two implementations, BRISK uses two pyramids for scale space representation. As shown in Fig. 4.1, the first one corresponds to the n octaves (denoted as c_i) of the scale space, and the second one corresponds to the n intra-octaves (denoted as d_i). In the first pyramid, it takes the original image as the first layer, and then the rest layers are derived by successively half-sampling the previous layers. It is similar for the second pyramid, whose first layer is obtained by downsampling the original image by a factor of 1.5. In this way, one can get a not-so-coarse scale space of the original image while still maintaining the effectiveness of computation. Meanwhile, as we will describe later, the scale of a keypoint is actually computed by interpolation in scale intervals, so such a not-very-fine scale space representation could still accurately locate keypoints in scale space.

To detect stable keypoints across scales, BRISK resorts to FAST feature detector for its efficiency and defines a FAST score for each candidate point as the saliency measure, which will be used in non-maximum suppression of candidate points. First, the FAST 9–16 detector (it identifies a keypoint by testing consecutive 9 points among 16 circular sampling points around a pixel) is applied on all octaves and intra-octaves to identify a set of candidate keypoints with a threshold T. For each candidate keypoint, a FAST score is then computed. The FAST score of a candidate keypoint is defined as the maximum threshold under which this point can be detected. Then,

Fig. 4.1 The scale space representation used in BRISK. It consists of two pyramids, whose images are reduced half by half along with layers. One corresponds to the octaves, while the other corresponds to the intra-octaves. The first octave is taken as the original input image, and the first intra-octave is obtained by downsampling the original image by a factor of 1.5

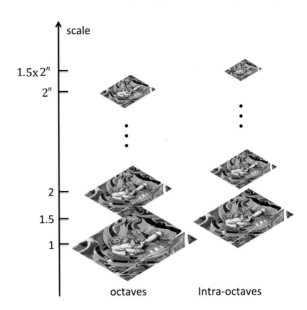

for each candidate keypoint, non-maximum suppression is applied by comparing its FAST score to those of its neighbors. For efficiency, it first examines whether its score is higher than its eight neighbors in the same scale layer. After fulfilling this condition, it checks the neighbors in the above and below layers. Since the images in different layers have different size, the FAST scores of neighbors in the above and below layers are obtained by interpolation. Finally, for those keypoints after non-maximum suppression, an efficient refinement process is used to get the subpixel keypoints along with their continuous scales.

In order to limit the complexity of this refinement process, three refined FAST scores are first computed from the current, the above and the below layers, respectively, by fitting a 2D quadratic function to the 3×3 neighborhood used in non-maximum suppression and taking the maxima. Then, these FAST scores along with their scales are used to fit a parabola, from which the refined scale of keypoint is computed as the peak position. Accordingly, the keypoint position on the refined scale is obtained by interpolation.

One special case that one has to deal with is detecting keypoints in the first octave, i.e., the original image which corresponds to scale 1. Obviously, for the first octave, there is no below layer available for scale refinement. In this case, BRISK applies the FAST 5–8 detector on the original image and obtains FAST scores as a 'virtual' layer below the first octave. Note that in this special case, BRISK does not require the FAST score of a keypoint in the first octave to be higher than its neighbors in the 'virtual' below layer. The 'virtual' below layer is just used in fitting a parabola for scale refinement.

(a)   (b)   (c)

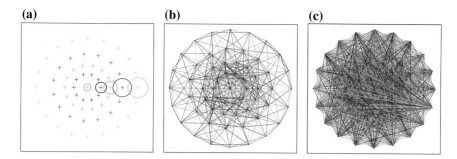

Fig. 4.2 **a** The sampling pattern used in BRISK. There are 60 sampling points (*including the central one*) regularly scattered on four concentric *circles* around the keypoint. Each sampling point consists of a position and a Gaussian kernel used to smooth its intensity. For clarity, only one sampling point from one circle is illustrated with its Gaussian kernel size (denoted by a *circle* around the sampling point) since all sampling points in a *circle* have same Gaussian smooth kernel. **b** The short-distance pairs of sampling points used for constructing descriptor. **c** The long-distance pairs of sampling points used for computing orientation. Each *color* indicates a pair

4.3.2 Orientation Assignment and Keypoint Description

Both computing a keypoint orientation and constructing binary descriptor for a keypoint are based on a sampling pattern shown in Fig. 4.2. This sampling pattern contains 60 sampling points, whose intensities are obtained by applying Gaussian smoothing[1] to avoid aliasing effects. The standard deviation of Gaussian kernel of a sampling point is proportional to its distance to the keypoint. Given these $N = 60$ sampling points, there are $N(N - 1)/2 = 1770$ point pairs. According to their distances, two subsets, a set of short-distance pairs $\mathbb{S}$ and a set of long-distance pairs $\mathbb{L}$, can be further obtained, as shown in Fig. 4.2b, c, respectively. Mathematically,

$$\mathbb{S} = \{(p_i, p_j) | \, \|p_i - p_j\| < \delta_{\max}\} \tag{4.5}$$

$$\mathbb{L} = \{(p_i, p_j) | \, \|p_i - p_j\| > \delta_{\min}\} \tag{4.6}$$

where $\delta_{\max}$ and $\delta_{\min}$ are set to 9.75δ and 13.67δ, respectively, and δ is the scale of keypoint.

Since the local gradients computed by those short-distance pairs tend to eliminate each other, the keypoint orientation defined on the averaged local gradient in this case will be unstable. As a result, the long-distance pairs are used to compute the keypoint orientation. It is defined as the orientation of the averaged local gradient obtained by these point pairs. The averaged local gradient is computed by:

---

[1]In the implementation of BRISK, it actually uses a box filter instead of the Gaussian filter. Smoothing by box filters with different sizes can be computed efficiently based on integral image, on the contrary to the time-consuming Gaussian smoothing with different kernels.

$$(g_x, g_y) = \frac{1}{n} \sum_{(p_i, p_j) \in \mathbb{L}} g(p_i, p_j) \tag{4.7}$$

$$g(p_i, p_j) = (I(p_i, \sigma_i) - I(p_j, \sigma_j)) \frac{p_i - p_j}{\|p_i - p_j\|^2} \tag{4.8}$$

where $I(p_i, \sigma_i)$ denotes the smoothed intensity at p_i and n is the number of long-distance pairs. Thus, the keypoint orientation is obtained by $\theta = \mathrm{atan2}(g_y, g_x)$. Note that to make the computed orientation relate to keypoint scale, the long-distance point pairs are scaled according to the keypoint scale.

Finally, according to the scale and orientation of a keypoint, its binary descriptor is obtained by comparing intensities among scaled and rotated short-distance point pairs, which can be done efficiently by prebuilding lookup tables. With the above sampling pattern and the short-distance pair threshold δ_{max}, there are 512 point pairs in $\mathbb{S}$, resulting a bit string of length 512 as BRISK descriptor.

4.4 FREAK: Fast Retina Keypoint

Although ORB and BRISK have improved BRIEF a lot to deal with scale and rotation changes while achieving even better matching performance, the FREAK proposed by Alahi et al. [1] in CVPR'12 goes beyond. It further improves the description and matching times of BRISK by a half and one-third, respectively. FREAK also won the Open Source Award in CVPR'12.

One point different from its predecessors is that FREAK does not contain a keypoint detector; it is only about how to efficiently extract and match binary descriptors for given keypoints, even though it does have a method to compute the local orientation for a keypoint to achieve rotation invariant feature description. Usually, it is used along with the BRISK keypoint detector as reported in its evaluations [1].

4.4.1 Descriptor Construction

The basic idea of FREAK about constructing binary descriptor is identical to BRISK. Both of them obtain a bit string as descriptor by comparing intensities between pairs of sampling points after Gaussian smoothing. The difference lies in the design of the sampling pattern. As shown in Fig. 4.3, FREAK also uses a sampling pattern with sampling points scattered on concentric circles as those in BRISK (cf. Fig. 4.2). However, FREAK samples point more densely near the keypoint, making the density of sampling points to drop exponentially as they are being far from the keypoint. Meanwhile, the size of Gaussian kernels used to smooth intensities of the sampling points is increased exponentially with respect to the distance to the keypoint. Such a sam-

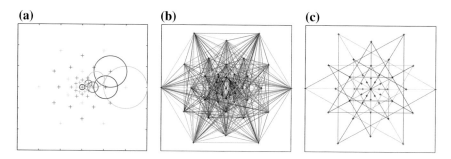

Fig. 4.3 **a** The sampling pattern used in FREAK. There are 43 sampling points regularly scattered on seven concentric *circles* around the keypoint. Each sampling point consists of a position and a Gaussian kernel used to smooth its intensity. For clarity, only one sampling point from one circle is illustrated with its Gaussian kernel size (denoted by a *circle* around the sampling point) since all sampling points in a *circle* have same Gaussian smooth kernel. Note that there exists orientation shift between two sampling points in the neighboring circles. **b** The pairs of sampling points used for constructing descriptor. **c** The pairs of sampling points used for computing orientation. Each *color* indicates a pair

pling pattern makes sampling points contain overlap information which is claimed to be more discriminative. What is more, FREAK uses the learning algorithm proposed in ORB (i.e., Algorithm 1) to select point pairs from all possible pairs generated from the sampling points. This is different from the strategy adopted in BRISK, which selects point pairs according to their distances. Finally, 512 point pairs shown in Fig. 4.3b are selected for constructing FREAK descriptor. No further improvement is observed with more point pairs according to Alahi et al.'s experiments [1].

For orientation computation, both BRISK and FREAK are based on the averaged local gradient computed from several point pairs, but these pairs are selected according to different rules. In BRISK, these point pairs are taken as those point pairs whose distances are larger than a certain threshold. While in FREAK, they are taken as those pairs which are symmetric with respect to the center of the sampling pattern (i.e., the keypoint). As shown in Fig. 4.3c, this strategy results in much fewer point pairs that are involved, so accelerating the computation speed.

4.4.2 Saccadic Matching with FREAK

It is noted by Alahi et al. that their FREAK descriptor is actually a coarse-to-fine descriptor, which mimics the saccadic search when human looks a scene. Specifically, the FREAK descriptor is equally divided into four parts according to the orders that they are selected in the learning algorithm. Each part contains 128 bits. In the matching stage, for a query feature, it first searches the database using the first 128 bits. Then, it only needs to continue comparison by the next bits only when the distance is smaller than a given threshold. Usually, more than 90 % candidates will be discarded using the first 128 bits. As a result, such a cascade of comparison could accelerate the matching step even further compared to directly matching by binary descriptors, e.g., BRISK. Interestingly, the divided four groups of bits based on the learning algorithm exhibit a similar structure to the human retina. For the point pairs in the first group, most of them are from the sampling points far away from the keypoint. On the contrary, for those point pairs in the last group, most of them are from the high density area of the sampling pattern.

4.5 FRIF: Fast Robust Invariant Feature

To achieve real-time feature detection, most methods refer to FAST and its variants. However, their detected feature points are less stable compared to the blob points detected based on second-order statistic [15, 18]. The main disadvantage of using second-order statistic, for example, Laplacian of Gaussian (LoG), lies in computational speed. It does not meet the requirement raised by real-time feature detection. Although SIFT [17] uses Difference of Gaussian (DoG) to approximate LoG and gains a speedup, it is still a non-realtime detector. To address this problem, Wang et al. [32] proposed to factorize LoG into a linear combination of rectangular filters, whose responses can be efficiently computed by integral image. With this approximation, it can detect stable feature points extremely fast based on the approximated LoG responses. Their feature detector is named Fast Approximation of LoG (FALoG) based on this motivation.

4.5.1 FALoG Detector

Since LoG is a continuous operator, it has to be approximated by a discrete template so as to obtain its responses on all pixels of an image. As an example to illustrate the basic idea of FALoG detector, in Fig. 4.4, a 9×9 template is used to approximate a LoG with Gaussian standard deviation of 1.2. This 9×9 template is further factorized into the sum of four rectangular templates with different weights. With this factorization, computing the responses of the approximated LoG filter over all pixels in an image can be efficiently done by summing over the responses of these rectangular filters, which can be computed rapidly using the integral image technique described in Sect. 2.2.

To obtain scale invariant keypoints, FRIF implements a scale space in a same way to BRISK [14]. Two pyramids containing octaves and intra-octaves are computed from the original image and the downsampled image, respectively. The downsampling factor is set to 1.5 so that the first intra-octave has a scale 1.5 times of the first octave. Interlacing these two pyramids constructs a scale space of the original image, whose odd layers are constituted by octaves in the first pyramid while even layers are from intra-octaves in the second pyramid. As a result, the scale in the $(2i + 1)$th layer is $\sigma_{(2i+1)} = 2^i \times \sigma, i = 0, 1, \ldots$, and the scale in the $2i$th layer is

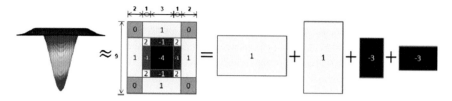

Fig. 4.4 A LoG (Laplacian of Gaussian) template can be decomposed into linear combination of several *rectangular* templates

$\sigma_{2i} = 1.5 \times 2^i \times \sigma, i = 1, 2, \ldots$. σ is the scale corresponding to the utilized LoG template, e.g., $\sigma = 1.2$ for a 9×9 template and $\sigma = 2$ for a 15×15 template.

Once the scale space has been constructed, FRIF computes integral images for all layers in the scale space, which can be accomplished very fast by scanning over the scale space only one time. Then, based on these integral images, the FALoG scores can be efficiently computed for all positions in all layers according to the factorization illustrated in Fig. 4.4. A threshold t is applied on FALoG scores to filter out positions with weak scores. For the remaining positions, non-maximum suppression and keypoint refinement are applied. Similar to BRISK, FRIF first checks whether the candidate keypoint has the largest FALoG score among its neighbors in the current layer. It goes to the above and below layers for further checking only if the candidate keypoint passes the test in the current layer. For the refinement, it first computes three refined FALoG scores for the current, the above and the below layers by fitting a 2D quadratic function to its neighbors in these three layers, respectively. Then, the three refined scores and their scales are used to fit a parabola from which the peak position is taken as the refined scale. Finally, the refined position corresponding to the refined scale of this keypoint is obtained by interpolation.

It is obvious that using such a scale space representation will encounter a same problem in detecting keypoint in the first layer as in BRISK, i.e., there is no below layer used for scale refinement. The solution is similar too. In the implementation of FRIF, it uses a 15×15 LoG template to compute FALoG scores in the scale space, and uses a 9×9 template on the original image to compute the scores as a 'virtual' layer below the first layer.

As in other LoG detectors (such as SIFT), it is necessary to remove those keypoints which are poorly located along edges. For this purpose, FRIF relies on thresholding the ratio of principal curvatures to remove this kind of keypoints. Similar to SIFT, the ratio of principal curvatures is obtained by the trace and determinant of the Harris matrix, which is computed on the corresponding scale space image.

4.5.2 Mixed Binary Descriptor

For orientation assignment and keypoint description, FRIF uses a similar sampling pattern to BRISK, as shown in Fig. 4.2. The difference is that FRIF assigns larger

Gaussian standard deviations to the sampling points far from the center. There are some overlaps among sampling points as this kind of arrangement is proven to be effectiveness in FREAK [1]. For point pairs generated from the sampling points, they are divided into short-distance pairs and long-distance pairs as BRISK does. The long-distance pairs are used for orientation assignment by computing the averaged local gradient (Eq. 4.7).

To obtain a M bit string as binary descriptor, FRIF proposes a different scheme to its predecessors (BRISK, ORB, FREAK, etc.). It only partly relies on the intensity comparison of the generated point pairs. Complementary to the intercomparison between sampling points, FRIF explores the local information around a sampling point. The underlying idea is motivated by LIOP [31] introduced in Sect. 3.3. For each sampling point, it first samples four points equally on a circle of radius R centered at this sampling point.[2] The smoothed intensities of these four sampling points (the smoothed Gaussian standard deviation is identical to its central point) are compared to each other, obtaining six bits. Therefore, we can totally obtain a $6N$ bit string, where N is the number of sampling points in the sampling pattern (cf. Fig. 4.2). For the remaining $M - 6N$ bits, FRIF resorts to the intensity comparisons between short-distance point pairs as a complementary information. The shortest $M - 6N$ point pairs are used as suggested by the authors' experiments [32]. Therefore, for a 512 bits binary descriptor, with a typical value of $N = 60$, it has to select 152 shortest point pairs. Since this kind of binary descriptor contains both intensity comparisons between sampling point pairs and local neighbors around a sampling point, it is named Mixed Binary Descriptor in FRIF.

4.6 Learning Binary Descriptors by Supervised Information

Learning binary descriptors by supervised information is becoming more and more popular due to its superior performance [5, 7, 25]. In fact, many previously introduced binary descriptors in this chapter have already utilized the idea of learning. For example, ORB and FREAK are based on an unlabeled dataset to learn high variance and less correlated bits. This kind of unsupervised learning has also been used in LDB (Local Difference Binary) [35] and OSRI [33] introduced in Sect. 3.4. Using labeled matching pairs and nonmatching ones, it is possible for one to learn a compact binary descriptor while maintaining high discriminative ability. With the supervised information, the authors of LDB have shown a better performance [36] than using unsupervised learning based on the same set of candidate bits. Similar improvement has also been observed in [5]. Basically, such methods can be classified into two

---

[2]Note that these circularly sampled points can be precomputed and stored for all sampling points in the sampling pattern, thus saving its run time in feature description.

categories: those built directly on image patch and those built on an intermediate representation of image patch (e.g., float-type feature descriptor).

4.6.1 From Raw Image Patch

For the first category, there are methods built on intensity or gradient, respectively. The former is usually very fast to compute, while the latter one is slower since extracting gradient related information needs additional time. However, learning binary descriptor on the basis of gradient could always lead to a better matching performance, due to the robustness of gradient. In what follows, we will first describe a computational efficient binary descriptor learned from the raw intensity patch. Then, we show how to learn more powerful and compact binary descriptor from the gradient information of patch.

4.6.1.1 Learning Binary Descriptor from Patch Intensity

Motivated by the high performance of subspace methods in feature extraction for face recognition [2, 10, 34], a straightforward idea to learn discriminative binary descriptor from patch intensity comes out to be first projecting the local image patch to a discriminant subspace and then thresholding the projected coordinates. Under this idea, given an image patch $x \in R^m$ which is denoted by a real-value vector made of its intensities, its binary descriptor can be obtained by:

$$b_i = sign(w_i^T x + t_i), i = 1, 2, \ldots, n \tag{4.9}$$

in which w_i is the ith projection and t_i is the threshold used in the ith projected coordinate. By denoting $W = [w_1 \ldots w_n] \in R^{m \times n}$ and $T = [t_1 \ldots t_n]^T \in R^n$, we can further have the n bits binary descriptor of x as $B(x) = sign(W^T x + T) \in \{0, 1\}^n$.

In the task of supervised learning, we could always have a set $\mathbb{P}$ of matching patch pairs (positives) and a set $\mathbb{N}$ of nonmatching patch pairs (negatives). The objective of learning a binary descriptor for image matching is to minimize the Hamming distances between matching pairs and at the meantime maximize the Hamming distances between nonmatching pairs using the learned binary descriptor. This goal can be directly formalized as solving the following maximization problem:

$$\max_{W,T} \frac{\sum_{(x,x') \in \mathbb{N}} \|B(x) - B(x')\|_2^2}{\sum_{(x,x') \in \mathbb{P}} \|B(x) - B(x')\|_2^2}$$
$$= \max_{W,T} \frac{\sum_{(x,x') \in \mathbb{N}} \|sign(W^T x + T) - sign(W^T x' + T)\|_2^2}{\sum_{(x,x') \in \mathbb{P}} \|sign(W^T x + T) - sign(W^T x' + T)\|_2^2} \tag{4.10}$$

$$s.t. \quad w_i^T w_j = 0, i \neq j$$
$$\|w_i\|_2 = 1$$

The orthogonal constraint imposed on projections has effect on reducing the redundancy across different dimensions and improving generalization of the learned projections [3, 11].

The sign function in this objective function makes it non-convex, so it is difficult to optimize the above problem directly. A typical and simple solution is to drop the sign function, therefore, we have the following optimization problem:

$$\max_{W} \frac{W^T \sum_{(x,x')\in\mathbb{N}} (x-x')(x-x')^T W}{W^T \sum_{(x,x')\in\mathbb{P}} (x-x')(x-x')^T W}$$
$$s.t. \quad w_i^T w_j = 0, i \neq j \qquad\qquad (4.11)$$
$$\|w_i\|_2 = 1$$

Note that by this relaxation, the threshold vector T is eliminated. Therefore, one has to learn these thresholds separately after finding the optimal projections. This can be achieved by a one-dimensional search which we will elaborate after showing how to obtain these optimal projections.

To get the optimal solution w_i of the above maximization problem, we can first obtain w_1 by solving the following subproblem:

$$\max_{w_1} \frac{w_1^T \sum_{(x,x')\in\mathbb{N}} (x-x')(x-x')^T w_1}{w_1^T \sum_{(x,x')\in\mathbb{P}} (x-x')(x-x')^T w_1}$$
$$s.t. \quad \|w_1\|_2 = 1 \qquad\qquad (4.12)$$

which can be solved by the standard eigenvalue decomposition technique. Denoting $A = \sum_{(x,x')\in\mathbb{N}} (x - x')(x - x')^T$ and $B = \sum_{(x,x')\in\mathbb{P}} (x - x')(x - x')^T$, w_1 is taken as the eigenvector corresponding to the largest eigenvalue of $Aw = \lambda Bw$.

Then, $w_i, i = 2, \ldots, n$ are computed iteratively by solving the following maximization problem with orthogonal constraints:

$$\max_{w} \frac{w^T A w}{w^T B w}$$
$$s.t. \quad w^T w_j = 0, j = 1, 2, \ldots, i - 1 \qquad\qquad (4.13)$$
$$\|w_i\|_2 = 1$$

Using the Lagrangian method, it can be shown that the solution of the above problem is equal to the largest eigenvector of the following eigenvalue problem:

$$((E - B^{-1} W_{i-1} (W_{i-1}^T B^{-1} W_{i-1})^{-1} W_{i-1}^T) B^{-1} A)w = \lambda w \qquad\qquad (4.14)$$

where E is the identity matrix and $W_{i-1} = [w_1 \ldots w_{i-1}]$ is the matrix formulated by the already obtained projections.

Now we show how to find the optimal thresholds $t_1, \ldots, t_n$ based on these projections. The basic idea is to obtain these thresholds one by one separately through optimizing its performance on the Hamming embedding of the training data. Although optimizing them together may lead to a better performance, the resulted combination problem is hard to solve. Moreover, the orthogonal constraint imposed on the projections lead to less redundance across dimensions. Therefore, solving t_i independently is a practical and reasonable solution.

In the binary case, if the larger one of a pair of projected data $w_i^T x, w_i^T x'$ is smaller than the threshold or the smaller one is larger than the threshold, this pair is considered to be a matching pair because they have identical bit values, either 0 or 1. Otherwise, it is classified as a nonmatching pair. Therefore, the true positive rate and the true negative rate at a given threshold t can be formulated as:

$$TP(t) = \Pr(u < t|\mathbb{P}) + \Pr(v \geq t|\mathbb{P})$$
$$TN(t) = \Pr(u \geq t \& v < t|\mathbb{N}) = 1 - \Pr(u < t|\mathbb{N}) - \Pr(v \geq t|\mathbb{N}) \tag{4.15}$$

where $u = \max\{w_i^T x, w_i^T x'\}$ and $v = \min\{w_i^T x, w_i^T x'\}$. By first computing TP and TN on a predefined set of t, and then searching t corresponding to the largest value of $TP + TN$, we can get the optimal t_i for the ith bit. One can also use the neighboring two positions along with the peak position to fit a parabola to get a better estimation of t_i.

In fact, the above method of learning and thresholding discriminant projections has also been used to the SIFT descriptor instead of raw intensity patch in LDAHash [24]. However, computing SIFT descriptor as a first step is computational expensive and impractical to some applications, especially the one required real-time processing. Considering the computational burden, directly applying discriminant subspace projection to patch intensity is also a bit high since it requires lots of time-consuming float-typed multiplications. To alleviate this problem, Trzcinski and Lepetit [28] proposed to approximate subspace projections by the linear combinations of a few efficient filters, for example, rectangular filters, box or Gaussian filters. Using rectangular filters, one can compute their responses very fast by integral image. While using box or Gaussian filters, their responses can be computed fast by convolution. Similar idea has also been explored in FRIF which is described in Sect. 4.5. Under this motivation, given a projection w_i, the objective is to reconstruct it by a predefined dictionary of efficient filters $D = [D_1 \ldots D_k]$:

$$\min_{\alpha_i} \|w_i - D\alpha_i\|_2^2 + \lambda \|\alpha_i\|_1 \tag{4.16}$$

The second term is a spare constraint, aiming to use as few filters as possible. Note that the strategy proposed here can be used to accelerate any linear projection operation.

For efficiency, supposing the local image patch is of size 32×32, the dictionary D is suggested to be chosen from the following strategies [28]:

(1) Rectangular filters: the dictionary is created by subsampling all possible rectangles available in the image patch. By considering the rectangles whose one edge is 1, 4, 7, 10, ..., a dictionary containing 34,596 elements is finally generated.
(2) Box filters: the dictionary is created by all 5×5 box filters centered at all pixels in the image patch. Thus, this dictionary contains 1,024 elements.

(3) Gaussian filters: it uses a similar way to generate this dictionary as in case of box filters. The difference is that here a Gaussian filter with $\sigma = 3$ is used instead of a 5×5 box filter.

4.6.1.2 Learning Binary Descriptor from Patch Gradient

Since gradient is more robust than intensity in general cases, researchers proposed binary descriptors by exploring gradient information. The standard pipeline of designing this kind of binary descriptor is to first generate a large set of candidate bits using gradient information, then using machine learning to select a few powerful bits as the binary descriptor.

Generating Candidate Bits: In the literature, the methods used to generate a bit feature on the basis of gradient have two types, either by comparing averaged gradients between two spatial grids [35, 36] or by thresholding the averaged oriented gradients over a spatial area [5, 26].

The first type is used in LDB, which is partially inspired by the pioneer work BRIEF. More specifically, the local image patch is first divided into 2×2, 3×3, 4×4, and 5×5 spatial grids. Then, the averaged intensity, horizontal gradient, and vertical gradient of each grid are computed. By comparing these values, respectively, for each pair of the spatial grids, three bits are obtained. Therefore, one can totally obtain a set of 1386 bits.

The second way to generate bit features is achieved by thresholding oriented gradients accumulated over a given spatial area, which is also known as pooling area or receptive field [5]. In other words, the candidate bits are defined by different receptive fields. Given a receptive field (R, c, t), which contains a spatial area R, an orientation c, and a threshold t, its corresponding bit feature can be computed by:

$$b(x; R, c, t) = sign \left(\frac{\sum\limits_{x \in R} g(x; c)}{\sum\limits_{i=1}^{N} \sum\limits_{x \in R} g(x; i)} - t \right) \qquad (4.17)$$

with

$$g(x; c) = \max(0, m(x) \cos(c - o(x))) \qquad (4.18)$$

where $o(x)$ and $m(x)$ are the gradient orientation and magnitude at x. $g(x; c)$ measures the gradient response on a predefined orientation c which is quantized in values of $\{0, \frac{2\pi}{N}, \ldots, (N-1)\frac{2\pi}{N}\}$.

Any type of spatial area can be used in the above bit feature. Due to the consideration of efficiency, rectangular, box, or Gaussian area is a good choice. This is because that accumulating values in these areas can be computed quickly which has been explained in Sect. 4.6.1.1. In [5], Fan et al. generated a very large pool of about

$3M$ candidate bits by emulating all possible rectangles in 64×64 image patch. They also generated a set of about $400K$ candidate bits by emulating all positions in the image patch with different Gaussian standard deviations: {0.5, 0.8, 1.2, 1.6, 2.0, 2.4, 2.8, 3.2, 3.6, 4.0, 4.4, 4.8, 5.6}.

Bits Selection by Supervised Learning: Generally, there are two kinds of learning strategies widely used in learning binary descriptors from the predefined candidate bit features. The first one is similar to that used in ORB (see Algorithm 1 in Sect. 4.2), but replacing the unsupervised measure of the goodness of a bit with a measure computed from labeled training data. For example, in [5], Fan et al. defined a goodness score based on the disparity of positive and negative samples, which is widely used in the Linear Discriminant Analysis [2]. For a given candidate bit, denoting m_1 and m_2 as mean values of bit differences between matching patch pairs and nonmatching pairs, respectively, and σ_1 and σ_2 as their corresponding variances, we can write a score as follows to measure how well this bit could separate matching pairs from nonmatching pairs:

$$s = \frac{(m_1 - m_2)^2}{\sigma_1 + \sigma_2} \tag{4.19}$$

The larger the s is, the better this bit could separate the positives and negatives in the training data.

AdaBoost [6] is a very powerful technique for feature selection, so it is natural to use it here as the second kind of learning strategy. Algorithm 2 gives a typical pipeline of Adaboost. Trzcinski et al. [27] have shown that by simply discarding the weight assigned to each weak learner, one can concatenate binary results of weak learner as a binary descriptor. Here, weak learners are those generated bits. In [36], Yang and Cheng pointed out that the original AdaBoost was proposed in a cascade manner, i.e., the latter bit is selected to deal with those samples that cannot be correctly classified in previous stages. This objective is a little different from that of feature matching, which is to separate positives and negatives by considering all the selected bits together. As a result, they proposed to modify Algorithm 2 with an alternative feature selection criterion. In each iteration, they select the bit with the smallest accumulated error instead of choosing the one with the smallest error in the current iteration. Note that as the number of selected bits increases, the remaining training samples are hard to be correctly classified by any remaining bit, and even the best accuracy is smaller than 0.5. In this case, continue the procedure of AdaBoost is meaningless because the following selected bits are no better than randomly selection. Using a very large training set is a direct solution. However, this strategy is extremely memory expensive and will slow down the learning procedure. It can be alleviated by sampling the training data in each iteration [25, 27]. Another solution is to use multiple smaller training sets and switch to a new training set when the selected bit has an accuracy smaller than 0.5 [36].

As demonstrated in Adaboost, many weak classifiers combined together can form a strong classifier. Inspired by this, Trzcinski et al. [25, 26] further enhanced the binary descriptor learned by Algorithm 2. Instead of using only one weak learner for each bit in the descriptor, they proposed to denote one bit by thresholding

---

Algorithm 2 Binary Feature Learning by AdaBoost

Input:
    A set of candidate bit features: $\mathbb{F} = \{b_1, b_2, \ldots, b_k\}$; a training set $\{X_i = (x_i, y_i, l_i), i = 1, \ldots, N\}$.

Output:
    A set of n bit features $\mathbb{B} = \{b_{(1)}, b_{(2)}, \ldots, b_{(n)}\}$.

1: Assign equal weights to all training data.
2: **for** $i = 1$ to n **do**
3:     Compute classification accuracy for all the candidate bits.
4:     Select the bit with the largest accuracy, denoted by $b_{(i)}$ and add it to $\mathbb{B}$.
5:     Compute the weight of $b_{(i)}$.
6:     Reweight all the training data according to the classification results of $b_{(i)}$. The sample that has been correctly classified decreases its weight, otherwise increases its weight. Normalize all the weights.
7: **end for**
8: **Output:** $\mathbb{B}$

---

linear combined responses of a set of weak learners. Formally, the proposed m-dimensional BinBoost descriptor is constituted by m sets of bit features, each of which contains n bits $\{b_{i1}, b_{i2}, \ldots, b_{in}\}$ selected from the feature pool and their corresponding weights $\{w_{i1}, w_{i2}, \ldots, w_{in}\}$. The resulting binary descriptor of an image patch x is then obtained by $C(x) = [c_1(x) \ldots c_m(x)] \in \{0, 1\}^m$, in which $c_i(x) = sign\left(\sum_{j=1}^{n} w_{ij} h_{ij}(x)\right)$ and $h_{ij}(x)$ denotes the binary response on x of the jth bit in the ith set.

Based on the above formulation of BinBoost descriptor, the related exponential loss optimized in AdaBoost is adapted to:

$$Loss = \sum_{i=1}^{N} \exp(-\gamma l_i \sum_{j=1}^{m} c_j(x_i) c_j(y_i)) \qquad (4.20)$$

where N is the number of training data.

One point different from the standard AdaBoost is that a constant weighting factor γ is used instead of different weights for different bits. This is particularly suitable to the task of binary descriptor learning as all bits in a binary descriptor are equally important in the utilized Hamming distance. However, this loss function is difficult to optimize because each bit is a thresholded linear combination of weak learner responses.

To efficiently learn these sets of weak learners as well as their weights, Trzcinski et al. [25] proposed a two-step greedy algorithm based on Adaboost. In each iteration, it first selects n bits from the candidate set of bit features by Algorithm 2, then optimizes the related weights by the Linear Discriminant Analysis. Note that the $c_k = sign\left(\sum_{j=1}^{n} w_{kj} h_{kj}(x)\right)$ minimizes the exponential loss at the kth iteration and also maximizes the following objective [23]:

$$\max_{w_{kj}} \sum_{i=1}^{N} l_i \alpha_k(i) c_k(x_i) c_k(y_i) \tag{4.21}$$

with

$$\alpha_k(i) = \exp(-\gamma l_i \sum_{j=1}^{k-1} c_j(x_i) c_j(y_i)) \tag{4.22}$$

By $\alpha_k(i)$, it assigns a higher weight to samples that are incorrectly classified by the previous selected bits, and a smaller weight to those correctly classified. Thus, it actually plays a role in changing weights of training samples to put more emphasize on harder ones in a similar spirit to AdaBoost.

Through relaxing $sign(x)$ as x, we can solve the following optimization problem to get w_{kj}:

$$\max_{W_k} \sum_{i=1}^{N} l_i \alpha_k(i) (W_k^T H_k(x_i))(W_k^T H_k(y_i))$$
$$= \max_{W_k} W_k^T \sum_{i=1}^{N} l_i \alpha_k(i) H_k(x_i) H_k^T(y_i) W_k \tag{4.23}$$

where $W_k = [w_{k1} \ldots w_{kn}]^T \in R^n$ and $H_k(x) = [h_{k1}(x) \ldots h_{kn}(x)]^T \in R^n$. By restricting $\|W_k\|_2 = 1$, the optimal W_k can be found as the eigenvector of the largest eigenvalue of $\sum_{i=1}^{N} l_i \alpha_k(i) H_k(x_i) H_k^T(y_i)$. The learning algorithm of BinBoost is summarized in Algorithm 3.

As a final remark, we have to point out that the binary selection methods described here are general, and not restricted to any kind of bit features although they were proposed initially with bit features generated from image gradient. In fact, Trzcinski et al. [26] have already shown the possibility of using the AdaBoost-based learning strategies for bit features generated by intensity comparison as BRIEF does.

Algorithm 3 BinBoost Learning of Binary Descriptor

Input:
   A set of candidate bits: $\mathbb{F} = \{b_1, b_2, \ldots, b_k\}$; a training set $\{X_i = (x_i, y_i, l_i), i = 1, \ldots, N\}$.
Output:
   m sets of n bit features $\mathbb{B}_i = \{b_{i1}, b_{i2}, \ldots, b_{in}\}, i = 1, \ldots, m$, m sets of n weights $\mathbb{W}_i = \{w_{i1}, w_{i2}, \ldots, w_{in}\}, i = 1, \ldots, m$.
1: Initialize training data with equal weight.
2: **for** $i = 1$ to m **do**
3:    Select n bits by the standard AdaBoost (Algorithm 2).
4:    Compute $\mathbb{W}_i = \{w_{i1}, w_{i2}, \ldots, w_{in}\}$ by solving (4.23).
5:    Compute weights of training samples according to Eq. (4.22) by the selected bits.
6: **end for**
7: **Output:** $\mathbb{B}_i$ and $\mathbb{W}_i, i = 1, \ldots, m$.

4.6.2   *From an Intermediate Representation*

For the second category, most of the existing methods can be summarized as first extracting a float-type feature descriptor (e.g., SIFT) from the local image patch and then applying hashing [30] or quantization [8] to obtain a bit string as the binary descriptor. Among these methods, the hashing-based method is predominant. Since the aim of this section is to introduce supervised learning approaches for binary descriptor, here we focus on supervised hash methods. It is worth to point out that LDAHash [24] is a typical hashing-based method that is dedicatedly proposed for local image matching, with application to large-scale image reconstruction and camera calibration. It uses the matching and nonmatching pairs of local patches as training data, so it directly optimizes errors on mismatches. On the contrary, other supervised learning to hash methods [7, 12, 16, 19, 29] have been well explored in the last decade and are mainly focused on preserving the initial distance characteristics of the float-type descriptors, with application to large-scale image recognition and retrieval. Some of them use pairwise supervised information, while others use sematic/class labels as supervised information. For the purpose of matching local interest regions (not matching at the image level), in most cases the available supervised information is given as the pairwise one, i.e., whether two samples are matched or not. As a result, not all hash methods are suitable. In what follows, we will introduce several representative ones that can be used for extracting local binary descriptors.

4.6.2.1   LDAHash

We represent a local image patch as $x \in \Re^n$, where x is an n-dimensional float-type representation of the patch. In [24], it uses SIFT. For convenience, we also represent a pair of patches as (x_i^1, x_i^2, l_i), in which $l_i \in \{0, 1\}$ is the label of this pair. $l_i = 1$ means this pair is constituted by two matching patches, and $l_i = 0$ means a nonmatching pair. The hash function used in LDAHash [24] is a linear projection followed by a threshold operation. Concretely, given a data x, it generates an m-bits code $y \in \{0, 1\}^m$ by $y = sign(W^T x + b)$, where $W \in \Re^{n \times m}$ is the projection matrix and $b \in \Re^m$ is the threshold vector. To find effective binary codes for matching, it is desirable that the binary codes of a matching pair should be as similar as possible, while the binary codes for a nonmatching pair should be as dissimilar as possible. Therefore, it minimizes the following objective function to find the optimal binary codes:

$$L(w) = \alpha E\left\{ \left\| y_i^1 - y_i^2 \right\|_2^2 |l_i = 1 \right\} - E\left\{ \left\| y_i^1 - y_i^2 \right\|_2^2 |l_i = 0 \right\} \qquad (4.24)$$

where E denotes expectation.

The above object function is hard to be optimized due to the sign function involved in y. LDAHash relaxes it by an approximation of $sign(x) = x$, as a result, the objective function becomes,

$$\tilde{L}(w) = \alpha E \left\{ \left\| W^T x_i^1 - W^T x_i^2 \right\|_2^2 \mid l_i = 1 \right\} - E \left\{ \left\| W^T x_i^1 - W^T x_i^2 \right\|_2^2 \mid l_i = 0 \right\}$$
(4.25)

Similar to the case of learning efficient linear projections for binary descriptor described in Sect. 4.6.1.1, this relaxation eliminates the threshold vector used for binary code generation. Therefore, after finding the optimal projection matrix, it is estimated by an one-dimensional search. Please see Sect. 4.6.1.1 for more details.

For learning the optimal linear projections, here, the objective function is a litter different from that used in Sect. 4.6.1.1. The relaxed objective function in Eq. (4.25) can be rewritten as,

$$\tilde{L}(w) = \alpha \, trace\{W^T A W\} - trace\{W^T B W\}$$
(4.26)

where

$$A = E\{(x_i^1 - x_i^2)(x_i^1 - x_i^2)^T \mid l_i = 1\} = \sum_{l_i=1}(x_i^1 - x_i^2)(x_i^1 - x_i^2)^T$$
(4.27)

$$B = E\{(x_i^1 - x_i^2)(x_i^1 - x_i^2)^T \mid l_i = 0\} = \sum_{l_i=0}(x_i^1 - x_i^2)(x_i^1 - x_i^2)^T$$
(4.28)

Strecha et al. [24] proposed two methods for minimizing Eq. (4.26): by minimizing $trace\{W^T A B^{-1} W\}$ or $trace\{W^T (\alpha A - B)\}$, whose solution is the m smallest eigenvectors of $A B^{-1}$ or $(\alpha A - B)$. With a proper value of α, the later one is slightly better according to the experimental results reported in [24].

4.6.2.2 Kernel-Based Supervised Hahsing

Kernel trick has been shown to be effective in tackling linearly inseparable data theoretically and empirically. Motivated by this, some researchers proposed to use kernel function to construct hash functions to generate binary code from real-valued input data [12, 13, 16]. Among them, KSH (Kernel-based Supervised Hashing) proposed by Liu et al. [16] is an effective and efficient one with elegant objective function for learning these hash functions.

Given a data $x \in \Re^n$, its ith bit in the corresponding binary code can be computed by the following hash function:

$$f_i(x) = sign\left(\sum_{j=1}^{K} w_{ij}\kappa(x_{(j)}, x) - b^i\right)$$
(4.29)

where $x_{(j)}, j = 1, \ldots, K$ are K anchor points uniformly sampled from the training set, $w_{ij}, j = 1, \ldots, K$ are K coefficients for the ith hash function and b^i is the bias. To make the generated bit take as much information as possible, it is expected that its mean value is 0 [22] (supposing a bit is 1 or -1). For this purpose, a good choice of b^i is the median of $\{\sum_{j=1}^{K} w_{ij}\kappa(x_{(j)}, x_1), \ldots, \sum_{j=1}^{K} w_{ij}\kappa(x_{(j)}, x_N)\}$ where N is the number of training samples. However, adopting the median will make the objective function too complex to optimize, so, using the mean value is a good alternative, i.e., $b^i = \frac{1}{N}\sum_{k=1}^{N}\sum_{j=1}^{K} w_{ij}\kappa(x_{(j)}, x_k)$. Therefore, the hash function in Eq. (4.29) becomes

$$
\begin{aligned}
f_i(x) &= sign\left(\sum_{j=1}^{K} w_{ij}\kappa(x_{(j)}, x) - \frac{1}{N}\sum_{k=1}^{N}\sum_{j=1}^{K} w_{ij}\kappa(x_{(j)}, x_k)\right) \\
&= sign\left(\sum_{j=1}^{K} w_{ij}(\kappa(x_{(j)}, x) - \frac{1}{N}\sum_{k=1}^{N}\kappa(x_{(j)}, x_k))\right)
\end{aligned}
\tag{4.30}
$$

By denoting $w_i = [w_{i1}, \ldots, w_{iK}]^T \in \mathfrak{R}^K$ and $\bar{\kappa}(x) = [\kappa(x_{(1)}, x) - \mu_1, \ldots, \kappa(x_{(K)}, x) - \mu_K] \in \mathfrak{R}^K$ where $\mu_k = \frac{1}{N}\sum_{i=1}^{N}\kappa(x_{(k)}, x_i)$, $f_i(x)$ can be simplified as $f_i(x) = sign(w_i^T \bar{\kappa}(x))$. The purpose of KSH is to leverage supervised information to learn parameters of m hash functions, making the resulted binary descriptor discriminative. For a data x, given the learned $w_i, i = 1, \ldots, m$, its binary descriptor can be computed by $h(x) = [f_1(x), \ldots, f_m(x)] \in \{-1, 1\}^m$. Here, for convenience of deriving the following objective function, we assume that a bit has a value of either 1 or -1, instead of 1 or 0. For two binary descriptors $h(x_i)$ and $h(x_j)$, their Hamming distance and inner product have the following relationship:

$$
h(x_i) \circ h(x_j) = m - 2D_H(h(x_i), h(x_j))
\tag{4.31}
$$

in which $D_H()$ denotes the Hamming distance.

For the task of learning local descriptor, the available label about the data is whether two samples are matched or not. In other words, denoting s_{ij} as the label of two samples, it means x_i and x_j are two matched samples when $s_{ij} = 1$, and $s_{ij} = -1$ means two nonmatched samples. For those pairs of samples with unknown similar/dissimilar relationship, $s_{ij} = 0$. An ideal result of learning is that the matched samples have the minimal Hamming distance (0) and the nonmatched samples have the maximal Hamming distance (m). According to the relationship shown in Eq. (4.31), we can obtain the following objective function for learning hash functions,

$$
\min_{w_i, i=1, \ldots, m} \| HH^T - mS \|_F^2
\tag{4.32}
$$

where $H = [h(x_1), \ldots, h(x_N)]^T \in \{-1, 1\}^{N \times m}$ is constituted by the binary codes of all samples. By denoting $X = [\bar{\kappa}(x_1); \ldots; \bar{\kappa}(x_N)] \in \mathfrak{R}^{N \times K}$, Eq. (4.32) is rewritten as:

$$
\min_{w_i, i=1, \ldots, m} \left\| \sum_{i=1}^{m} sign(Xw_i)sign(Xw_i)^T - mS \right\|_F^2
\tag{4.33}
$$

To solve the above optimization problem, Liu et al. [16] proposed a greedy method, which solves w_i iteratively. For the ith iteration, let us assume that the coefficients for the previous solved hash functions are $w_1^*, \ldots, w_{i-1}^*$. Then, the coefficients for the ith hash function can be obtained by solving the following objective function:

$$\min_{w_i} \left\| sign(Xw_i)sign(Xw_i)^T - S_{i-1} \right\|_F^2 \qquad (4.34)$$

where $S_{i-1} = mS - \sum_{t=1}^{i-1} sign(Xw_t^*)sign(Xw_t^*)^T$ is the residual error after obtaining $(i-1)$ hash functions. $S_0 = mS$. Through mathematical operations and discarding the constant term, solving Eq. (4.34) is equivalent to solve

$$\min_{w_i} -sign(Xw_i)^T S_{i-1} sign(Xw_i) \qquad (4.35)$$

Direct solving Eq. (4.35) is still difficult due to the existence of sign function. It is reasonable to approximate the sign function with the sigmoid function $\phi(x) = 2/(1 + exp(-x)) - 1$. As a result, we get the following minimization problem:

$$\min_{w_i} -\phi(Xw_i)^T S_{i-1} \phi(Xw_i) \qquad (4.36)$$

which can be solved by a standard gradient descend algorithm. The gradient is $\nabla = -X^T(S_{i-1}\phi(Xw_i)) \odot (1 - \phi(Xw_i) \odot \phi(Xw_i))$ in which $\odot$ is the Hadamard product.

The initial value of w_i for gradient descend can be obtained by a spectral relaxation to the original minimization problem in Eq. (4.35). It is to solve the following constraint quadric problem:

$$\begin{aligned} \max_{w_i} \quad & (Xw_i)^T S_{i-1}(Xw_i) \\ s.t. \quad & (Xw_i)^T(Xw_i) = N \end{aligned} \qquad (4.37)$$

The additional constraint makes the N elements in vector Xw_i fall into the range of $[-1,1]$ so that the solution of the relaxed problem is in the similar range to the original problem in Eq. (4.35). The relaxed problem in Eq. (4.37) can be solved by eigenvalue decomposition and taking w_i as the eigenvector of the largest eigenvalue of $X^T S_{i-1} Xw = \lambda X^T Xw$. The constraint is then satisfied by scaling the obtained eigenvector.

References

1. Alahi, A., Ortiz, R., Vandergheynst, P.: FREAK: Fast retina keypoint. In: IEEE Conference on Computer Vision and Pattern Recognition, pp. 510–517 (2012)
2. Belhumeur, P., Hepanha, J.P., Kriegman, D.J.: Eigenfaces vs. Fisherfaces: recognition using class specific linear projection. IEEE Trans. Pattern Anal. Mach. Intell. **19**(7), 711–720 (1997)

3. Cai, D., He, X., Han, J., Zhang, H.J.: Orthogonal laplacianfaces for face recognition. IEEE Trans. Image Process. **15**(11), 3608–3614 (2006)
4. Calonder, M., Lepetit, V., Ozuysal, M., Trzcinski, T., Strecha, C., Fua, P.: BRIEF: computing a local binary descriptor very fast. IEEE Trans. Pattern Anal. Mach. Intell. **33**(7), 1281–1298 (2012)
5. Fan, B., Kong, Q., Trzcinski, T., Wang, Z., Pan, C., Fua, P.: Receptive fields selection for binary feature description. IEEE Trans. Image Process. **23**(6), 2583–2595 (2014)
6. Friedman, J., Hastie, T., Tibshirani, R.: Additive logistic regression: a statistical view of boosting. Ann. Stat. **28**(2), 337–407 (2000)
7. Gong, Y., Kumar, S., Rowley, H.A., Lazebnik, S.: Learning binary codes for high-dimensional data using bilinear projections. In: IEEE Conference on Computer Vision and Pattern Recognition, pp. 484–491 (2013)
8. Gong, Y., Lazebnik, S.: Iterative quantization: a procrustean approach to learning binary codes. In: IEEE Conference on Computer Vision and Pattern Recognition, pp. 817–824 (2011)
9. Harris, C., Stephens, M.: A combined corner and edge detector. In: Alvey Vision Conference, pp. 147–151 (1988)
10. He, X., Yan, S., Hu, Y., Niyogi, P., Zhang, H.: Face recognition using laplacianfaces. IEEE Trans. Pattern Anal. Mach. Intell. **27**(3), 328–340 (2005)
11. Hua, G., Brown, M., Winder, S.: Discriminant embedding for local image descriptors. In: International Conference on Computer Vision, pp. 1–8 (2007)
12. Kulis, B., Darrell, T.: Learning to hash with binary reconstructive embeddings. In: Advances in Neural Information Processing Systems, pp. 1042–1050 (2009)
13. Kulis, B., Grauman, K.: Kernelized locality-sensitive hashing for scalable image search. In: International Conference on Computer Vision, pp. 2130–2137 (2009)
14. Leutenegger, S., Chli, M., Siegwart, R.: BRISK: Binary robust invariant scalable keypoints. In: International Conference on Computer Vision, pp. 2548–2555 (2011)
15. Lindeberg, T.: Feature detection with automatic scale selection. Int. J. Comput. Vis. **30**, 79–116 (1998)
16. Liu, W., Wang, J., Ji, R., Jiang, Y.G., Chang, S.F.: Supervised hashing with kernels. In: IEEE Conference on Computer Vision and Pattern Recognition, pp. 2074–2081 (2012)
17. Lowe, D.: Distinctive image features from scale-invariant keypoints. Int. J. Comput. Vis. **60**(2), 91–110 (2004)
18. Mikolajczyk, K., Schmid, C.: Indexing based on scale invariant interest points. In: International Conference on Computer Vision, pp. 525–531 (2001)
19. Norouzi, M., Fleet, D.J.: Minimal loss hashing for compact binary codes. In: International Conference on Machine Learning (2011)
20. Ojala, T., Pietikainen, M., Harwood, D.: A comparative study of texture measures with classification based on feature distributions. Pattern Recogn. **29**, 51–59 (1996)
21. Rosten, E., Drummond, T.: Machine learning for high speed corner detection. In: European Conference on Computer Vision, pp. 430–443 (2006)
22. Rublee, E., Rabaud, V., Konolige, K., Bradski, G.: ORB: an efficient alternative to SIFT or SURF. In: International Conference on Computer Vision, pp. 2564–2571 (2011)
23. Schapire, R.E., Singer, Y.: Improved boosting algorithms using confidence-rated predictions. In: Annual Conference on Computational Learning Theory, pp. 80–91 (1998)
24. Strecha, C., Bronstein, A.M., Bronstein, M.M., Fua, P.: LDAHash: improved matching with smaller descriptors. IEEE Trans. Pattern Anal. Mach. Intell. **34**(1), 66–78 (2012)
25. Trzcinski, T., Christoudias, M., Fua, P., Lepetit, V.: Boosting binary keypoint descriptors. In: IEEE Conference on Computer Vision and Pattern Recognition, pp. 2874–2881 (2013)
26. Trzcinski, T., Christoudias, M., Lepetit, V.: Learning image descriptors with boosting. IEEE Trans. Pattern Anal. Mach. Intell. **37**(3), 597–610 (2015)
27. Trzcinski, T., Christoudias, M., Lepetit, V., Fua, P.: Learning image descriptors with the boosting-trick. In: Advances in Neural Information Processing Systems (2012)
28. Trzcinski, T., Lepetit, V.: Efficient discriminative projections for compact binary descriptors. In: European Conference on Computer Vision, pp. 228–242 (2012)

29. Wang, J., Kumar, S., Chang, C.F.: Sequential projection learning for hashing with compact codes. In: International Conference on Machine Learning (2010)
30. Wang, J., Shen, H.T., Song, J., Ji, J.: Hashing for similarity search: a survey. CoRR (2014). arxiv.org/abs/1408.2927
31. Wang, Z., Fan, B., Wu, F.: Local intensity order pattern for feature description. In: International Conference on Computer Vision, pp. 603–610 (2011)
32. Wang, Z., Fan, B., Wu, F.: FRIF: Fast robust invariant feature. In: British Machine Vision Conference (2013)
33. Xu, X., Tian, L., Feng, J., Zhou, J.: OSRI: a rotationally invariant binary descriptor. IEEE Trans. Image Process. **23**(7), 2983–2995 (2014)
34. Yan, S., Xu, D., Zhang, B., Zhang, H.J., Yang, Q., Lin, S.: Graph embedding and extensions: a general framework for dimensionality reduction. IEEE Trans. Pattern Anal. Mach. Intell. **29**(1), 40–51 (2007)
35. Yang, X., Cheng, K.T.: LDB: An ultra-fast feature for scalable augmented reality on mobile devices. In: International Symposium on Mixed and Augmented Reality, pp. 49–57 (2012)
36. Yang, X., Cheng, K.T.: Local difference binary for ultrafast and distinctive feature description. IEEE Trans. Pattern Anal. Mach. Intell. **36**(1), 188–194 (2014)

Chapter 5
Visual Applications

Abstract Local image descriptors have been widely used in many computer vision applications such as 3D reconstruction, object detection and recognition, image stitch, image retrieval, and localization etc. to name a few. In this chapter, we will introduce some of them, and show how a robust and discriminative descriptor is used in these specific applications.

Keywords Local descriptor applications · Object recognition · SFM · 3D reconstruction · SLAM · Image retrieval

5.1 Structure from Motion and 3D Reconstruction

3D reconstruction, especially large-scale 3D reconstruction from hundreds of thousands of images, has attracted wide interest in the area of computer vision. A core and fundamental step in 3D reconstruction is to establish reliable point correspondences among images. With these correspondences, it is possible to recover the poses of cameras which captured these images as well as the 3D space points that these matching points correspond to based on the multi-view geometry [12] theory and robust estimation methods. As this process simultaneously involves recovering 3D space points (structure) and camera poses (motion), it is also known as structure from motion.

Figure 5.1 shows a typical pipeline of modern approach for scene/object 3D reconstruction from multiple images. It contains (sparse) feature matching, bundle adjustment of structure from motion (sparse reconstruction), and dense reconstruction using multi-view stereo techniques.

Feature Matching: The first step is to establish reliable point correspondences across images. Given a pair of images, feature matching contains three steps: (1) Detecting repeatable feature points from each image; (2) Assigning a local descriptor to each feature point; and (3) For each feature point in one image, searching for its two most similar feature points in the other image according to distances among descriptors. If the ratio of the nearest distance and the second nearest distance is below a threshold, this pair of points is declared as a match. Although many feature detectors and descriptors can be used, SIFT is a popular choice for its robustness and historical

© Springer-Verlag Berlin Heidelberg 2015
B. Fan et al., *Local Image Descriptor: Modern Approaches*,
SpringerBriefs in Computer Science, DOI 10.1007/978-3-662-49173-7_5

(a)   **(b)**

(c)   **(d)**

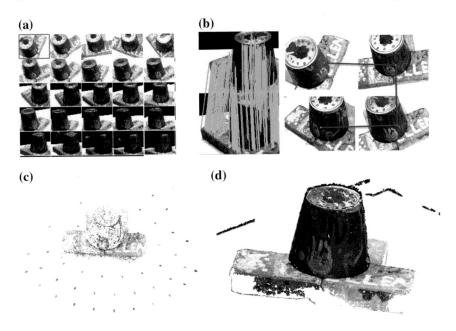

Fig. 5.1 A typical system of 3D reconstruction from **a** multiple images usually contains three steps of progressively, **b** feature matching, **c** structure from motion, and **d** dense reconstruction

reasons.[1] In the third step, using exhaustive matching of all feature points between two images is tolerable for tasks with a small number of images. However, in most cases, there are many images. Therefore, it is necessary to use a fast nearest neighbor search algorithm to do this job. The approximate nearest neighbors (ANN) [2] and KD-Tree [23] are popular choices. To obtain a set of reliable matching points, the initial matching results got by the nearest neighbor search are refined by estimating a fundamental matrix using RANSAC [8]. Then, the estimated fundamental matrix is further refined by applying Levenberg–Marquardt (LM) algorithm [28] on its eight parameters using the inliers obtained from RANSAC. Finally, matches with large fitting errors to the refined fundamental matrix are removed. If the remaining number of matches is less than a threshold, e.g., 20, all matches are removed and the two images are considered as nonoverlapping.

After obtaining a set of matching points for each pair, they are grouped into feature tracks by checking all matching points of all image pairs. A feature track is defined as a connected matching point across multiple images as depicted in Fig. 5.1b. Obviously, a feature track corresponds to a 3D point. Note that if one-to-one correspondence is not imposed in the feature matching stage, there may be more than one point in an

---

[1] In the time when the Photo Tourism [39] (a milestone work of large-scale image-based 3D reconstruction) was proposed, SIFT was still the best available technique for establishing point correspondences. The quality of feature matching achieved by SIFT is capable of reconstructing most scenes, so it is still a first choice up to now.

image are contained in a feature track. In this case, the feature track is removed as it is inconsistent. The remaining consistent feature tracks are used as input in structure from motion to recover their corresponding 3D points and camera poses.

Structure from Motion: Structure from motion aims to simultaneously estimate the camera poses and 3D points of the input feature tracks automatically. Under the pinhole camera model, and making the common additional assumptions that the pixels are square and the center of projection is the image center, a camera can be parameterized by seven parameters: three parameters for its 3D rotation matrix R, three parameters to denote its center C, and one parameter to denote its focal length f. Meanwhile, since many daily used cameras and lenses usually produce images with noticeable distortion, it is necessary to consider this distortion in the camera imaging model. Therefore, two additional parameters κ_1, κ_2 are used to model the radial distortion.

Although there are nine elements in a 3D rotation matrix, it only has three degrees of freedom. For numerical robustness, the camera rotation R is usually parameterized in an incremental way, i.e., $R = \Delta(\Omega)R \cdot \Omega = [w_x w_y w_z]^T$ is the parameter vector which will be optimized in each iteration, and the updating rotation matrix $\Delta(\Omega)$ is expressed using Rodriguez formula:

$$\Delta(\Omega) = I + \sin\phi[\Omega]_\times + (1 - \cos\phi)[\Omega]_\times^2 \tag{5.1}$$

in which $\phi = |\Omega|$ and

$$[\Omega]_\times = \frac{1}{\phi}\begin{bmatrix} 0 & -w_z & w_y \\ w_z & 0 & -w_x \\ -w_y & w_x & 0 \end{bmatrix} \tag{5.2}$$

Besides the Rodriguez formula, quaternions [31] and geometric algebra [15] are two other ways for representing the incremental rotation.

Together with other six parameters, each camera can be represented by a nine vector: $\Theta = [\Omega, C, f, \kappa_1, \kappa_2]$. According to the camera model, a 3D point X is projected onto a 2D point m in an image by progressively transforming X to homogeneous image coordinate X', performing perspective division and applying radial distortion. With the camera Θ, this process can be formulated as follows:

$$X' = R(X - C) \tag{5.3}$$

$$P' = -f[X_1'/X_3', X_2'/X_3'] \tag{5.4}$$

$$\rho^2 = \left(\frac{P_1'}{f}\right)^2 + \left(\frac{P_2'}{f}\right)^2 \tag{5.5}$$

$$m = (\kappa_1\rho^2 + \kappa_2\rho^4)P' \tag{5.6}$$

For convenience, we denote the above process by a mapping function $m = P(X; \Theta)$. Suppose there are n images captured for 3D reconstruction, n cameras $\Theta_i, i = 1, \ldots, n$ need to be estimated. After feature matching, we will have k feature tracks, each of which corresponds to a 3D point X_i that needs to be estimated. Each feature track contains a set of image coordinates, m_{ij} denotes the image coordinate observed in the ith camera of the jth feature track. Since the purpose of structure from motion algorithm is to recover camera parameters $\Theta_i, = 1, \ldots, n$ and 3D points $X_i, i = 1, \ldots, k$ by minimizing the reprojection errors, we can write its objective as:

$$\min_{\{\Theta_i, X_j\}} \sum_{i=1}^{n} \sum_{j=1}^{k} l_{ij} \left\| m_{ij} - P(X_j; \Theta_i) \right\| + \lambda(\kappa_1^2 + \kappa_2^2) \tag{5.7}$$

where l_{ij} is an indicator variable to indicate whether the ith camera observes the point X_j ($l_{ij} = 1$) or not ($l_{ij} = 0$). The second term acts as a regularizer to prohibit large radial distortions.

Solving this problem is also known as bundle adjustment, for which the LM algorithm is a popular choice. However, the LM algorithm is only guaranteed to find local minima. As a result, to avoid the risk of getting stuck in bad local minima, in addition to give a good initialization, it is reasonable to solve it in an incremental way, each time adding one or several cameras.

The algorithm is started by estimating camera parameters and 3D points for two images. To make sure the initial reconstruction is reliable, the selected two images should have a large baseline and a large number of matches. For this purpose, a common strategy is to fit a homography between each matching image pair using RANSAC and record the inlier percentage. The image pair with the lowest inlier percentage and has at least 100 matches is then used for the initial two-frame reconstruction, which is accomplished by first estimating camera parameters (e.g., using five-point algorithm [26]) along with triangulation from available matches and then refined by bundle adjustment.

Then, multiple cameras are added to the optimization in each round. As the current reconstruction is available, the image with the largest number of matches that have been triangulated can be found from the remaining images, and added to the optimization. Other images with at least 75 % of the largest number of such matches are added too.

For a new added image, its camera parameters are estimated by direct linear transform algorithm (DLT) [12] based on the correspondences of recovered 3D points and their projections on this image. These parameter values are used as an initialization for a following bundle adjustment step, in which only the parameters of new camera and 3D points it observes are optimized. After this bundle adjustment step, the new 3D points observed in the new camera are added into the optimization of the whole model. Note that only the points which are observed by at least one other recovered camera and triangulate them is robust are added. For a point in the new image, all its corresponding points in other recovered images along with itself are used to generate rays from camera centers to the points respectively. The largest angle of all pairs of rays is used to decide if this point can be triangulated robustly or not. If this angle is larger than a threshold (usually set to be $2°$), it is a good point. After adding new 3D points, all the camera parameters and 3D points are refined by re-running the bundle adjustment. To improve robustness, it is necessary to remove unreliable feature tracks that contain at least one image coordinate with high reprojection error. Once again, after removing unreliable feature tracks, optimization is re-run. These two steps are iterative until no more feature tracks are removed. Finally, this procedure is repeated for all the added images, and then adding more images until no image can be added. Figure 5.1c gives a typical result of structure from motion.

Dense Reconstruction: The recovered 3D points by structure from motion are usually very sparse, as depicted in Fig. 5.1c. This is because that the 3D points generated by structure from motion are obtained through triangulation of matching keypoints which are sparsely distributed in images. However, such sparse distributed 3D points are not enough to generate a 3D model of the photographed object/scene in most cases. Therefore, a step of dense reconstruction is required after structure from motion. It usually takes the images along with their recovered camera parameters as input.

There are several kinds of multi-view stereo methods to achieve this goal, including voxel-based methods [33, 35], deformable polygonal meshes [7, 9], methods based on multiple depth maps [14, 37], and patch-based methods [10, 18, 36]. Among them, patch-based methods have some properties that make them better than others. First, they do not require any other information such as the bounding box or the initial disparity range etc. which are required by other kinds of methods. Second, they are simple and effective. As a result, patch-based methods are popular choice in an automatical 3D reconstruction system from multiple images.

Figure 5.2 illustrates the basic idea explored in patch-based methods. For a pixel in one image, we first hypothesize several depths along its viewing ray which is determined by the camera parameters. Then for each hypothesized depth, the algorithm checks the photometric discrepancy of a local window around the pixel and its corresponding windows in other visible images. This discrepancy is the minimal and its value will be extremely small for the true depth. By optimizing over this depth almost for every pixel in all images, one can obtain a highly dense set of 3D points.

For the patch-based methods, the recently proposed Patch-based Multi-View Stereopsis (PMVS) [10] has been widely used in modern 3D reconstruction systems, such as the one described in [1]. It contains the three steps of initial feature matching, patch expansion, and patch filtering. The initial matching is to obtain an initial set of reconstructed patches/3D points by triangulating corresponding Harris/DoG keypoints justified by epipolar geometry. Patch expansion and filtering are iterated several times to get dense patches and remove erroneous ones. The rule for patch expansion is based on the assumption that nearby patches should have similar normal vectors and adjacent patch centers. The patch filtering aims to remove unreliable patches by checking visibility consistency and smooth constraint.

Finally, we have to point out that there are many excellent open resources for 3D reconstruction from multiple images. Both the structure from motion algorithm used

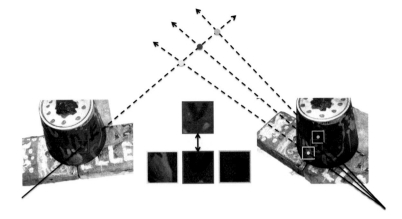

Fig. 5.2 The basically underlying rule used in multi-view stereo algorithms. For a point in one image, it first hypothesizes several depths along the ray from the camera to the image point shown in *green*, *red*, and *yellow circles*. These depths are reprojected into other images to check the local photometric consistency to find the correct depth, shown with *red color*

in Photo Tourism [39] and PMVS [10] have source codes available on the Internet.[2] Meanwhile, 'VisualSFM' is a good software integrating all necessary steps of 3D reconstruction, which can be downloaded from http://ccwu.me/vsfm/.

5.2 Object Recognition

In computer vision community, the task of recognizing objects is generally considered to cover two types: *specific object* recognition and *generic object* recognition.

Specific object recognition is also referred as instance recognition in some literature, because it aims to identify instances of a very concrete and already known object in images. For example, a particular toy, a book cover, and so on. The objects need to be recognized are usually stored as image templates in a database. As shown in Fig. 5.3a, the main challenges for specific object recognition include geometric changes such as viewpoint and scale changes, occlusion, and cluttered background.

While for the generic object recognition which is also known as category recognition, its purpose is to identify instances of an object in the category level, such as face, cat, building, chair, etc. The instances recognized by a generic object recognition algorithm only have to share a similar high-level concept, and it is not necessary for them to be belonging to a same concrete object. Besides the difficulties encountered in specific object recognition, generic object recognition has to conquer other

---

[2]The Bundler software used in Photo Tourism for structure from motion can be downloaded from http://www.cs.cornell.edu/~snavely/bundler/.
The PMVS is available on http://www.di.ens.fr/cmvs/.

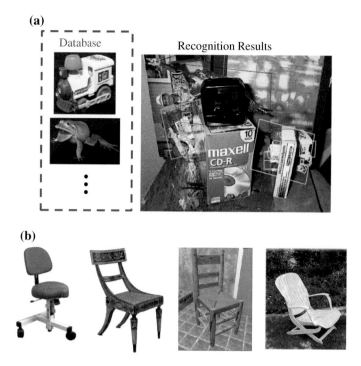

Fig. 5.3 Object recognition contains two different tasks in general. **a** Specific object recognition aims to find out instances of concrete objects stored in database; **b** generic object recognition is to recognize objects belonging to a same conceptual category. For instance, the listed four chairs are actually from different instances, but they belong to a same category

challenges caused by different appearance and variable shape configurations that exist in different instances of objects from the same conceptual category. Figure 5.3b shows some instances belonging to the same category, from which we can find significant variations in their appearances and shapes.

Local descriptors play an important role on both of them, but in different ways. Briefly speaking, in specific object recognition, local descriptors are used to find reliable matches between the objects in database and the input image to accumulate evidence for the existence of a specific object. While in generic object recognition, local descriptors extracted in an image are used to achieve a robust global representation of the image, which is further fitted to a predictable model of the studied category.

Specific Object Recognition: Until now, the most powerful paradigm for specific object recognition is still the one proposed by Lowe [21] in 1999, in which the initial version of SIFT was proposed. It includes two typical steps of matching local feature points and geometric verification as shown in Fig. 5.4. Concretely, given a query image as input, it first detects keypoints and constructs their local descriptors in the input image. Then, it matches the detected keypoints to those stored in the

Fig. 5.4 The standard pipeline used in computer vision for specific object recognition. It relies on matching of detected keypoints (indicated as *green circles*) and geometric verification (the *red rectangle* indicates the recognized object)

database according to their descriptor distances. Finally, based on the established point correspondences between the input image and the stored object images in the database, geometric verification is applied to filter out false positives as well as to further determine the location and pose of the recognized object in the input image.

In the first step, both float type and binary descriptors introduced in previous chapters can be used. When using float point descriptors, it is usually used along with a fast indexing technique, e.g., KD-Tree [23], in order to accelerate matching. While for binary descriptors, although matching a pair of them is fast by Hamming distance, it is still necessary to utilize hashing technique for fast matching due to the large-scale database. For example, the database contains lots of objects that we want to recognize. In case of only one or several objects, using brute force matching of binary descriptors is a better choice as hashing binary descriptors will decrease the performance.

In geometric verification, since there are mismatches in the obtained matching set, it has to accurately estimate the underlying geometric transformation while simultaneously be robust to outliers. For this purpose, Generalized Hough Transform [21] and RANSAC [8] as well as its variants are popular choices. Concerning the transformation model, although perspective transformation is more general for rigid object, using affine transformation is enough in most practical cases.

Generic Object Recognition: As can be seen from the above, specific object recognition is more or less a problem of image matching. For the generic object recognition, the basic principal is largely different from that in specific object recognition. It often includes learning a statistical model on the global representation (can be appearance, texture, shape or their combination) of image based on a training set per category. By the learned model, it can make predictions for object presence or localization in newly unseen images. Compared to specific object recognition, recognition of generic object is more challenging as it is more general and there exists even larger intraclass variance than interclass variance.

As an example system of generic object recognition, we describe the popular bag of visual words image classification framework. It was first proposed by Csurka et al. [5], and then dominates the methods for generic image classification until very recently. Bag of visual words is actually a technique for holistic image representation. With this kind of representation, a simple SVM classifier (often along with a kernel, such as the χ^2-kernel) is trained for each category and used for deciding whether a test image belongs to this category or not.

In the bag of visual words representation, there are three main steps: feature extraction, feature encoding and feature pooling. Initially, a vocabulary is generated by clustering feature descriptors extracted on a given set of images [27, 38]. Each cluster center is taken as a visual word. Then for each image in the training set, feature descriptors are computed either on detected keypoints or densely sampled pixels. Although any local descriptor can be used, SIFT is an extremely popular choice. Based on the previous generated vocabulary, each feature is encoded into a vector whose dimension is the size of vocabulary, i.e., the number of visual words. The state-of-the-art feature encoding methods are Locality-constraint Linear Coding (LLC) [40], Localized Soft-assignment Coding (LSC) [19], and Fisher Kernel [29, 30]. Finally, these encoded vectors are pooled together by spatial pyramid pooling [16], obtaining a vector as the holistic representation of the input image. In spatial pyramid pooling, either using max pooling (take the maximal element in a spatial region) or sum pooling (take the sum in a spatial region) is related to the feature encoding method. For example, it has been shown that max pooling will result in a better performance with LLC and LSC, while the sum pooling is better when using the original hard assignment.

One remark about this kind of methods is that although it is mainly reported to operate on an image-level in the literature, it is natural to use it on window-level as well. In this case, the model is trained with the holistic representations of objects within bounding boxes and tested with a sliding window scan. However, when the resolution of an object in image is too low, it is not suitable.

5.3 Content-Based Image Retrieval

A content-based image retrieval system aims to return a number of most similar images to the query image from a very large database, which usually contains more than 100,000 images. The idea is to help users to quickly find out images having similar content to what they have from a very large database. Depending on the application scenery, the input query may be a whole image or an interest region in an image indicating the interesting part/object, as shown in Fig. 5.5.

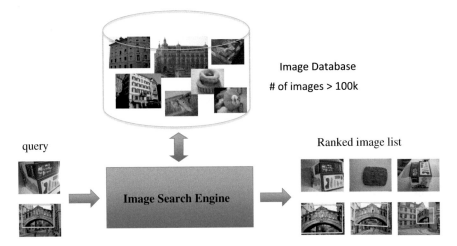

Fig. 5.5 A content-based image retrieval system takes image as query, and outputs a ranked list of images in the database that are similar to the query image in content. For a retrieval system, the size of database is huge, for example, larger than 100k images. There are usually two types of queries: image or interest region/object in an image

While the principal technique in such systems is reliable image matching across a database, the abilities to scale well to very large database and process in a short time lie in the heart of it. Therefore, the utilized technique is different from that in specific object recognition,[3] although they share some similar points in concept. In this part, we will introduce how to build a popular image retrieval system based on the bag of visual words representation of image and fast feature indexing techniques.

First, as described in the part of "Generic Object Recognition," the first step is to determine a vocabulary for bag of visual words representation. Different from object recognition or image classification task, the size of vocabulary is usually much larger in case of large-scale image retrieval, often 2–3 orders of magnitude larger than that used in object recognition. For example, using a vocabulary with 1,000,000 visual words is an usual setup for image retrieval system, while the size of vocabulary is around several thousands in most cases for object recognition. Meanwhile, due to the huge number of images in database, the number of local descriptors used to generate visual words is huge too. Such a huge size of data and the number of clusters make the simple k-means algorithm [6] and other popular clustering algorithms (e.g., mean-shift [4] and spectral clustering [25]) infeasible. Both the hierarchical k-means [27] and the approximate k-means [32] have good scalability to big data, but approximate k-means has shown a better performance according to Philbin et al.'s retrieval experiments [32]. The idea of approximate k-means is to replace the step of exact nearest neighbor search for each cluster in each iteration by approximate nearest neighbor search. Since the exact nearest neighbor search takes

---

[3]In the task of specific object recognition, the database storing object images is usually not very large.

most of computation in k-means, this replacement largely reduces the computational burden. For approximate nearest neighbor search, any available algorithm is feasible. In [32], a forest of eight randomized k-d trees is used. By using approximate nearest neighbor search, the computational complexity in each iteration of k-means reduces from $O(NK)$ to $O(Nlog(K))$ where N is the number of data (local descriptors) used for clustering and K is the number of clusters (visual words). Considering the large value of K, the reduction is noticeable.

Second, for each image, local descriptors are computed from keypoints (or interest regions) detected on this image. Then, given the generated vocabulary, these local descriptors are considered together to obtain a vector representation of the image, whose dimension equals to the size of the vocabulary. More specifically, each element of this vector representation records the number of local descriptors in this image that belong to the corresponding visual word. A local descriptor is belonged to the nearest visual word in the vocabulary according to the distances between descriptors and visual words. To make this representation independent of the number of local descriptors in different images, it is further normalized by dividing each dimension with the total number of local descriptors in the image. Inspired by the text retrieval system [3], besides the word frequency, a weight considering the importance of the corresponding visual word is also applied. These two factors constitute the so-called tf-idf (term frequency-inverse document frequency) weighting strategy [3, 38]. In an image, if a visual word appears very often, it should be assign a large weight. Meanwhile, if a visual word appears mostly in all images, it means that this word has low discriminative ability, so its weight should be small. These two points are the underlying principals of the tf-idf weighting strategy. To sum up, the tf-idf weight of a visual word is proportional to its frequency in an image, and inversely proportional to its frequency of appearing in images of the whole dataset.

Once the tf-idf weighted bag of visual words representations have been computed for all images in the database, given a query image, one can compute its vector representation according to the above procedure. Then, by searching for its n nearest neighbors in the database, one can return its top n similar images. Obviously, exhausted search is time consuming and infeasible considering the size of the database. The usually used techniques for fast approximate nearest neighbor search, such as k-d tree and locality sensitive hashing, are less efficient due to the extremely high dimension of the image representation. Here, analogy to the inverted file indexing in text information retrieval, an alternative but straightforward strategy is used for indexing such high dimensional vectors [32]. The key observation is that the bag of visual words representation is highly sparse because of the very large vocabulary size (e.g., 1 million) and the relatively small number of local descriptors detected in an image (several thousands). Therefore, these visual words have already quantized the database. As a result, one only needs to search for nearest neighbors from a subset of the database, which is constituted by the images having visual words appeared in the query image. In implementation, each visual word contains a list of image IDs along with their corresponding tf-idf weights assigned to this visual word. For each image in the obtained subset, the distance between its tf-idf weight and that of the query image is accumulated for all appeared visual words in the query image,

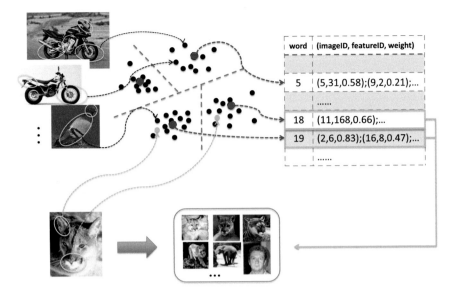

Fig. 5.6 Illustration of vocabulary generation for local descriptors and the inverted file indexing strategy used for image retrieval

so the obtained distance is identical to explicitly computing it. The output images are sorted according to this distance in an ascending order. Figure 5.6 illustrates this efficient strategy for indexing. We have to point out that this strategy is only efficient when the vocabulary size is much greater than the number of local descriptors in one image.

Optionally, one can check geometric consistency of the correspondences established between the query image and the returned image, and then rerank the returned image list according to the geometric verification. This additional step can improve the retrieval accuracy and is mandatory if the objective is to output the localization of the interest region/object in images. However, the query time will increase too, but it is still in a reasonable range because only the top-ranked images (for example, 1000 most similar images returned by indexing of bag of visual words) are needed to check for geometric consistency. Meanwhile, the algorithm used for this purpose is quite efficient. For each image returned by the previous step, the feature correspondences between it and the query image can be obtained by Lowe's second nearest neighbor distance ratio test [20, 22]. In this case, the k-d tree can be used for fast nearest neighbor search. As the following geometric verification is robust to outliers (incorrect correspondences), here an extremely fast search strategy can be used instead of matching local descriptors. This is achieved in a similar way to the inverted file indexing used for retrieving similar images. For a local feature in the query image, its possible corresponding features in one returned image are those features belonging to the same visual word. For one possible correspondence, it can estimate a simple geometric transformation from it and use the estimated transformation to get a set of inliers by checking all possible correspondences. Then, all the inliers are used to estimate a finer transformation (e.g., affine transformation). This procedure is iterated through all possible correspondences and the best transformation with the largest number of inliers is kept. Based on the inlier numbers, the returned images are reranked. For the simple geometric transformation used in the first stage, a transformation of "translation+isotropic scale" is enough to get a good performance. This transformation can be quickly computed from one correspondence using the features' centers and scales. Philbin et al. [32] evaluated other transformations including "translation+anisotropic scale" and "translation+vertical shear" and found that the final performance difference is very small. This may because that the followed finer transformation estimation evens out the differences used in the first stage. Besides the inlier number, another score that can be used to rerank images is the sum of idf weights of the visual words which inlier correspondences belong to. This is because that the idf measures how importance a visual word is, so by summing up all idf weights for the geometric verified visual words, it indicates the geometric consisted similarity.

5.4 Simultaneous Localization and Mapping (SLAM)

SLAM is a task for reconstructing environment and localizing itself in real time. It is a highly desirable capability for a robot to explore an unknown place. There are different types of SLAM based on different sensors, such as laser, LiDar, and camera. Among them, the video-based monocular SLAM has high potential for the mass-market, both in navigation for unmanned vehicles/aircrafts and augmented reality applications. In this part, we will introduce a state-of-the-art monocular SLAM system, which can operate in various practical environments, from small to large, and indoor to outdoor ones. Its name is ORB-SLAM [24], because it uses ORB feature [34] as its core element.

ORB-SLAM is a multithread-based system, whose architecture is illustrated in Fig. 5.7. Different from the well-known PTAM [13] which contains two threads for tracking and mapping, respectively, it contains three threads, with one additional thread for loop closing. The first thread is processed every frame, while the latter two are processed when a new keyframe is added. Their functions are summarized in the follows:

* *Tracking thread.* It processes every frame taken from the camera. This thread is in charge of estimating the camera pose and inserting new keyframes by tracking the local map. The camera pose can be estimated from the previous frame, or by global relocalization if the tracking is lost in the previous frame. Global relocalization is performed by place recognition based on bag of visual words (more precisely, bag of binary words [11], in which ORB is used). Since the system is designed with a keyframe culling strategy that is implemented in the mapping thread, the policy for inserting keyframes is generous whenever it is possible.

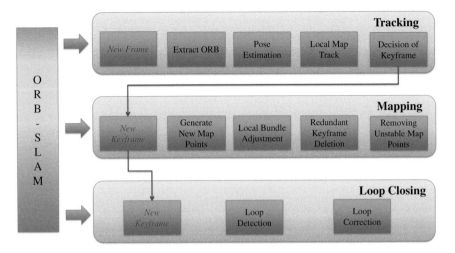

Fig. 5.7 System overview of the ORB-SLAM. It contains three threads in charge of tracking, mapping, and loop closing, respectively. See the text for details

- *Mapping thread.* This thread is activated when a keyframe is detected and inserted into the system. It generates new map points (3D points) from the new keyframe by triangulating ORB features from connected keyframes. It also uses local bundle adjustment to refine the poses and the map points related to the new keyframe and its connected keyframes, as well as to discard outlier map points. Meanwhile, in this thread, it checks for the quality of visible map point and remove unstable ones. Finally, the mapping thread is responsible for detecting and removing redundant keyframes. This is important for maintaining a compact reconstruction and enables long-term operation.
- *Loop closing thread.* It takes the last keyframe processed by the mapping thread. The task of this thread is to detect and close loops by querying loop candidates from a database and computing the related similarity transformation.

After initializing the system, the tracking thread is running all the time, dealing with every frame. For the mapping thread and the loop closing thread, they are idle in most time and activated by the tracking thread when a new keyframe is detected and inserted into the system. In what follows, we will elaborate modules used in these three threads.

Extract ORB features: To deal with scale changes, ORB features are extracted at 8-scale levels with a scale factor of 1.2. Meanwhile, to make the extracted features distribute homogeneous in image coordinate, image is divided into grid with equal size. Except for the grids from which no ORB feature point can be detected due to the low contrast and textureless, 1000 feature points are regularly scattered among these grids by adapting the detector threshold in each grid. If some grids do not have enough feature points, the remaining points are equally assigned to other grids similarly. These features are used for reconstructing map points, pose estimation, tracking map points, searching for similar keyframes for place recognition, etc.

Pose estimation: According to whether the tracking is lost in the previous frame or not, there are two different ways for pose estimation. In the first case, if the tracking was successful for the last frame, the initial camera pose is predicted based on the constant velocity motion assumption. A guided search of ORB feature points in the current frame is performed for the map points observed in the last frame. Then, the pose is optimized with the found 3D to 2D correspondences. In the second case, namely the tracking is lost, pose estimation is performed by global relocalization. More specifically, the current frame is represented by bag of binary words as described in [11] and used to query a recognition database which is constituted by added keyframes incrementally. For each returned keyframe, its map points are matched to feature points in the current frame by comparing their ORB descriptors. The RANSAC incorporated with the PnP algorithm [17] is used to estimate the camera pose. Then a guided search of more matches to the map points in the keyframe is performed, followed by an optimization with the found correspondences. Finally, we take the best pose estimation with the largest inliers. If this number of inliers is larger than a threshold, global relocalization is successful and the tracking procedure continues.

Local map tracking: After pose estimation, we can project a local map around the current frame into the current frame to obtain more point correspondences. With a local map, the computational complexity is reduced as we do not need to search for all map points, most of which are actually not visible in the current frame. The local map is constituted by map points from the keyframes that share map points with the current frame and their neighboring (connected) keyframes.[4] Each map point in these keyframes is searched in the current frame for correspondences by checking some properties with the current frame's camera pose, including the projection point, the projection viewing ray, the distance to camera center, the scale and distance between the related ORB descriptors. With this enlarged set of point correspondences, the camera pose can be further refined.

Decision of new keyframe: To make the tracking robust to challenging camera movements, we should insert keyframe as fast as possible. However, this strategy will result in a fast increasing amount of keyframes which can prohibit the long-term operation of SLAM. Fortunately, in ORB-SLAM, it also contains a keyframe culling strategy to stop the number of keyframes grows unbounded. The current frame is inserted as a keyframe if less than 90% map points in its reference keyframe[5] is tracked in the current frame and it simultaneously fulfills the following conditions: (1) More than 20 frames have passed since the last global relocalization which is important for a good relocalization; (2) At least 50 points are tracked in the current frame which ensures a good tracking; and (3) The mapping thread is idle or more than 20 frames have passed since the last keyframe insertion.

---

[4]A keyframe is defined to be connected to another when the number of their common map points exceeds a predefined threshold.

[5]A reference keyframe of a frame is the keyframe shares most map points with the frame.

Generate new map points: For each unmatched ORB feature in the newly inserted keyframe, we search for its corresponding feature in one of its connected keyframes. Then, using RANSAC with the epipolar constraint to filter out outliers, and the inliers are triangulated to obtain new 3D points. After checking the depth direction in both cameras, parallax, reprojection error, and scale consistency, the remaining 3D points are added to the map. These newly added map points are searched for correspondences in the rest of connected keyframes as described in the local map tracking module.

Local bundle adjustment: Local bundle adjustment is used to optimize the camera poses of the newly inserted keyframe along with its connected keyframes, and the map points observed in these keyframes as well as the newly generated ones. For those keyframes that observe map points but not in the connected set of keyframes, they are included in the optimization but remain fixed. As in 3D reconstruction application, the Levenberg–Marquadt algorithm is used for bundle adjustment. After the local bundle adjustment, the outlier map points are discarded.

Keyframe culling: Detecting and removing redundant keyframes is an important characteristic of ORB-SLAM, because this prohibits the number of keyframes grows unbounded and enables it to operate in long term. The culling strategy is simple. If one keyframe has more than 90% map points that are also observed in at least three connected keyframes, it is discarded.

Map points culling: For a newly generated map point, it has to be observed from the first three keyframes after creation and must be tracked in more than 25% of the frames in which it is predicted to be visible. Otherwise, it will be discarded. After the first three keyframes, a map point will be removed whenever it is observed from less than three keyframes, which might happen when keyframes are culled and the local bundle adjustment discards outlier observations.

Loop detection: Loop detection aims to recognize a previously visited place, i.e., a place recognition problem. For this purpose, the last processed keyframe is represented by bag of binary words, and is compared to all of its connected keyframes. Among these, the smallest similarity score is recorded as s_{min}. Then, the last keyframe is used to query a database constituted by the previously added keyframes, only keeping the keyframes whose similarity scores are higher than s_{min}. Meanwhile, all the keyframes that are connected to the last keyframe are excluded too. In the remaining keyframes, if there exist at least three connected keyframes, each of them is taken as a loop candidate and called loop keyframe.

Loop correction: Based on the detected loop location, loop correction is to correct the accumulated error and distribute it equally to all connected path. First of all, a similarity transformation between the current keyframe and the loop keyframe is to be computed based on 3D correspondences with RANSAC. These 3D correspondences are established through matching ORB descriptors related to the map points in these keyframes. If the number of inliers is larger than a threshold, a guided search is performed for more correspondences. With the enlarged set of correspondences, the similarity transformation is optimized again. The system accepts this loop if this similarity transformation is supported by enough inliers. Once the similarity transformation is obtained, the poses of the current keyframe and its connected keyframes can be corrected. Meanwhile, duplicated map points observed in the current keyframe and the loop keyframe as well as its connected keyframes can be fused. To this end, all the map points in the loop keyframe and its connected keyframes are projected into the current keyframe and searching for their matched points by the method described in the "local map tracking" module. All these matched points along with the inliers in similarity transformation estimation are fused.

The final remark about the above-described SLAM system is initialization, which aims to compute the relative pose between two frames to triangulate an initial set of map points to start the SLAM process. While many SLAM methods use an interactive initialization, the ORB-SLAM is able to initialize itself automatically when a good two-view configuration is achieved. As depicted in Fig. 5.8, the automatic initialization algorithm contains five steps. First, feature correspondences are obtained by detecting and matching ORB features in two frames. Then, they are used to estimate a homography and a fundamental matrix parallel by RANSAC, followed by a model selection to decide which one is better suited for the current two frames. With the selected model (homography or fundamental matrix), several motion hypotheses are recovered and the best one is selected by checking the configurations of the triangulated 3D points, most of which should be seen with parallax, in front of both cameras and with low reprojection errors. Finally, bundle adjustment is used to refine the camera pose and the 3D points to obtain the initial map.

Fig. 5.8 The automatic initialization approach utilized in ORB-SLAM

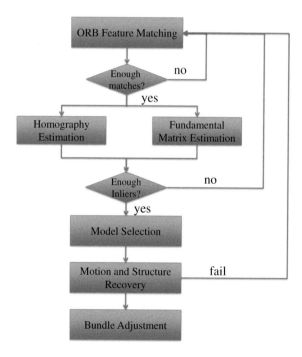

References

1. Agarwal, S., Snavely, N., Simon, I., Seitz, S., Szeliski, R.: Building Rome in a day. In: International Conference on Computer Vision, pp. 72–79 (2009)
2. Arya, S., Mount, D.M., Netanyahu, N.S., Silverman, R., Wu, A.Y.: An optimal algorithm for approximate nearest neighbor searching fixed dimensions. J. ACM **45**(6), 891–923 (1998)
3. Baeza-Yates, R., Ribeiro-Neto, B.: Modern Information Retrieval. ACM Press (1999)
4. Cheng, Y.: Mean shift, mode seeking, and clustering. IEEE Trans. Pattern Anal. Mach. Intell. **17**(8), 790–799 (1995)
5. Csurka, G., Bray, C., Dance, C., Fan, L.: Visual categorization with bags of keypoints. In: European Conference on Computer Vision Workshop on Statistical Learning in Computer Vision, pp. 1–16 (2004)
6. Duda, R.O., Hart, P.E., Stork, D.G.: Pattern Classification (2nd Edition). Wiley-Interscience (2000)
7. Esteban, C.H., Schmitt, F.: Silhouette and stereo fusion for 3d object modeling. Comput. Vis. Image Underst. **96**(3), 367–392 (2004)
8. Fischler, M.A., Bolles, R.C.: Random sample consensus: a paradigm for model fitting with applications to image analysis and automated cartography. Commun. ACM **24**(6), 381–395 (1981)
9. Furukawa, Y., Ponce, J.: Carved visual hulls for image-based modeling. Int. J. Comput. Vis. **81**(1), 53–67 (2009)
10. Furukawa, Y., Ponce, J.: Accurate, dense, and robust multiview stereopsis. IEEE Trans. Pattern Anal. Mach. Intell. **32**(8), 1362–1376 (2010)
11. Galvez-Lopez, D., Tardos, J.: Bags of binary words for fast place recognition in image sequences. IEEE Trans. Robot. **28**(5), 1188–1197 (2012)
12. Hartley, R., Zisserman, A.: Multiple View Geometry. Cambridge University Press (2004)
13. Klein, G., Murray, D.: Parallel tracking and mapping for small ar workspaces. In: International Symposium on Mixed and Augmented Reality, pp. 1–10 (2007)
14. Kolmogorov, V., Zabih, R.: Multi-camera scene reconstruction via graph cuts. In: European Conference on Computer Vision, pp. 82–96 (2002)
15. Lasenby, J., Lasenby, A.N., Doran, C.J.L., Fitzgerald, W.J.: New geometric methods for computer vision: An application to structure and motion estimation. Int. J. Comput. Vis. **26**(3), 191–213 (1997)
16. Lazebnik, S., Schmid, C., Ponce, J.: Beyond bags of features: spatial pyramid matching for recognizing natural scene categories. In: IEEE Conference on Computer Vision and Pattern Recognition, pp. 2169–2178 (2006)
17. Lepetit, V., Moreno-Noguer, F., Fua, P.: Epnp: An accurate O(n) solution to the PnP problem. Int. J. Comput. Vis. **81**(2), 155–166 (2009)
18. Lhuillier, M., Quan, L.: A quasi-dense approach to surface reconstruction from uncalibrated images. IEEE Trans. Pattern Anal. Mach. Intell. **27**(3), 418–433 (2005)
19. Liu, L., Wang, L., Liu, X.: In defense of soft-assignment coding. In: International Conference on Computer Vision, pp. 2486–2493 (2011)
20. Lowe, D.: Distinctive image features from scale-invariant keypoints. Int. J. Comput. Vis. **60**(2), 91–110 (2004)
21. Lowe, D.G.: Object recognition from local scale-invariant features. In: International Conference on Computer Vision, pp. 1150–1157 (1999)
22. Mikolajczyk, K., Schmid, C.: A performance evaluation of local descriptors. IEEE Trans. Pattern Anal. Mach. Intell. **27**(10), 1615–1630 (2005)
23. Muja, M., Lowe, D.G.: Scalable nearest neighbor algorithms for high dimensional data. IEEE Trans. Pattern Anal. Mach. Intell. **36**(11), 2227–2240 (2014)
24. Mur-Artal, R., Montiel, J.M.M., Tardós, J.D.: ORB-SLAM: a versatile and accurate monocular SLAM system. IEEE Trans. Robot. **31**(5), 1147–1163 (2015)
25. Ng, A.Y., Jordan, M.I., Weiss, Y.: On spectral clustering: analysis and an algorithm. In: Advances in Neural Information Processing Systems, pp. 849–856 (2001)

26. Nister, D.: An efficient solution to the five-point relative pose problem. IEEE Trans. Pattern Anal. Mach. Intell. **26**(6), 756–777 (2004)
27. Nistér, D., Stewénius, H.: Scalable recognition with a vocabulary tree. In: IEEE Conference on Computer Vision and Pattern Recognition, pp. 2161–2168 (2006)
28. Nocedal, J., Wright, S.J.: Numerical Optimization. 2nd Edition, Springer (2006)
29. Perronnin, F., Dance, C.: Fisher kernels on visual vocabularies for image categorization. In: IEEE Conference on Computer Vision and Pattern Recognition, pp. 1–8 (2007)
30. Perronnin, F., Sánchez, J., Mensink, T.: Improving the fisher kernel for large-scale image classification. In: European Conference on Computer Vision, pp. 143–156 (2010)
31. Pervin, E., Webb, J.A.: Quaternions for computer vision and robotics. In: IEEE Conference on Computer Vision and Pattern Recognition, pp. 382–383 (1983)
32. Philbin, J., Chum, O., Isard, M., Sivic, J., Zisserman, A.: Object retrieval with large vocabularies and fast spatial matching. In: IEEE Conference on Computer Vision and Pattern Recognition, pp. 1–8 (2007)
33. Pons, J.P., Keriven, R., Faugeras, O.: Multi-view stereo reconstruction and scene flow estimation with a global image-based matching score. Int. J. Comput. Vis. **72**(2), 179–193 (2007)
34. Rublee, E., Rabaud, V., Konolige, K., Bradski, G.: ORB: An efficient alternative to SIFT or SURF. In: International Conference on Computer Vision, pp. 2564–2571 (2011)
35. Seitz, S.M., Dyer, C.R.: Photorealistic scene reconstruction by voxel coloring. In: IEEE Conference on Computer Vision and Pattern Recognition, pp. 1067–1073 (1997)
36. Shen, S.: Accurate multiple view 3d reconstruction using patch-based stereo for large-scale scenes. IEEE Trans. Image Process. **22**(5), 1901–1914 (2013)
37. Shen, S., Hu, Z.: How to select good neighboring images in depth-map merging based 3d modeling. IEEE Trans. Image Process. **23**(1), 308–318 (2014)
38. Sivic, J., Zisserman, A.: Video Google: A text retrieval approach to object matching in videos. In: International Conference on Computer Vision, pp. 1470–1477 (2003)
39. Snavely, N., Seitz, S.M., Szeliski, R.: Photo tourism: exploring photo collections in 3D. ACM Trans. Graph. **25**, 835–846 (2006)
40. Wang, J., Yang, J., Yu, K., Lv, F., Huang, T., Gong, Y.: Locality-constrained linear coding for image classification. In: IEEE Conference on Computer Vision and Pattern Recognition, pp. 3360–3367 (2010)

Chapter 6
Resources and Future Work

Abstract In this chapter, we will first briefly introduce several benchmarks used for evaluating local image descriptors. They are organized based on different visual applications. Finally, to conclude this book, we would like to draw some remarks about the current status of this area, and describe some future directions according to the authors' opinions.

Keywords Evaluating local descriptors · Computer vision datasets and benchmarks · Online resources of local descriptors · Future work about local descriptors

6.1 Dataset and Evaluation Protocol

Dataset along with its related evaluation protocol constitutes a benchmark. Benchmark plays a significant role in algorithm development, because it makes different methods comparable based on a standard evaluation procedure and public available dataset.

Local image descriptor is widely used in various computer vision tasks, so there are many datasets and evaluation protocols toward different applications. In this chapter, we would like to give a brief introduction to some popular datasets as well as their evaluation protocols for image matching, object recognition, and image retrieval, respectively. Meanwhile, we will supply with some useful links to online resources.

6.1.1 Benchmarks for Image Matching

6.1.1.1 Oxford's VGG Dataset

This dataset contains 8 sets of image sequences, each of which contains 6 images with an increasing amount of geometric or photometric distortion. The transformations between these images include viewpoint change, scale change, image rotation, image blur, illumination change, and JPEG compression. It was first proposed by Mikolajczyk et al. for the purpose of evaluating matching performance of different local descriptors [27] and different affine interest regions [28]. Since then, it has become the most widely used dataset for newly proposed local descriptors until now.

The images in this dataset are either of planar scenes or the camera position is fixed during acquisition, so their relationship can be well modeled by a homography in all cases. In this dataset, along with the tested image pairs, their homographies are supplied too. As a result, the mapping relating images can be computed and used to determine groundtruth matches. Therefore, it is objective to compare local descriptors about their matching performance and compare feature detectors about their repeatability.

To evaluate local descriptors, the curve of "1-precision versus recall" is often used. The precision is defined as the ratio of correct matches and total matches, while the recall is defined as the ratio of correct matches and all possible feature correspondences which are obtained by a guided search of matching feature points based on the given groundtruth transformation. When the affine interest region is used, a correspondence is defined according to the overlap error, which measures how well two regions correspond under a homography. Given two regions A and B from two images, respectively, and H the homography between the two images, the overlap error is calculated by $\varepsilon = 1 - (A \cap H^T B H)/(A \cup H^T B H)$. If the overlap error is smaller than 50%, two regions are considered to be a feature correspondence. Another approach is to use the distance between the transformed pairs to define a correspondence, i.e., $dist(x_a, x_b) = \max(\|f(x_a; H) - x_b\|_2^2, \|x_a - f(x_b; H^{-1})\|_2^2)$, where $f(x; H)$ means transforming x according to the homography H, and x_a and x_b are two features from two images. If this distance is below a given threshold, for example, two pixels in most cases, x_a and x_b, are considered as a feature correspondence. By changing the threshold used for accepting a feature match, one can obtain a number of operation points (precision, recall) in this curve, thus drawing the curve.

In evaluation of feature detectors, repeatability score is the often used objective measurement. It is defined as the ratio of all possible feature correspondences and the minimal number of features in two images. Usually, only features in the common part of the scene presented in both images are taken into account. The definition of possible feature correspondence is identical to that used in the evaluation of feature descriptors.

This dataset and the related codes for performance evaluation are available on: http://www.robots.ox.ac.uk/~vgg/research/affine/. VLBenchmarks also reimplements this protocol and is available on: http://www.vlfeat.org/benchmarks/overview/repeatability.html

6.1.1.2 DTU Robot Image Dataset

This is a huge dataset collected by researchers in the Technical University of Denmark (DTU) for the purpose of two-view image matching [1]. It contains 135,660 images of 60 different scenes, acquired from 119 positions and 19 different illuminations. These scenes cover a wide range of material and reflectance properties, for example, fabric, fruits, vegetables, model house, wood branches, building material, art objects, etc. Along with these images of size 1200 × 1600, it supplies with calibration data of camera positions and poses as well as the groundtruth 3D surfaces of the imaged scenes which were obtained by a structured light scanner. Therefore, a potential image correspondence can be verified based on the known surface geometry and camera parameters. A similar dataset (3D Objects on Turntable) for evaluating performance of different detectors and descriptors on 3D objects was proposed in [30]. However, it uses epipolar constraints of three calibrated views to verify a potential feature correspondence. Since some mismatches can pass the test as well, it is not reliable compared to using both 3D surface and camera parameters for verification. Moreover, the DTU dataset contains more illumination changes than the 3D Objects dataset, and the scenes in DTU dataset are more complex.

Using this dataset, the performance measurements are similar to those used for the VGG dataset, i.e., curves formed by recall and precision. The dataset images, calibration data, groundtruth 3D surfaces, and the evaluation code can be downloaded from: http://roboimagedata.compute.dtu.dk/.

6.1.1.3 Patch Dataset

This dataset contains local image patches which have been scale and rotation normalized. In other word, there is a small scale change and in-plane rotation between any two matching patches. They mainly exhibit substantial perspective distortion caused by viewpoint changes and illumination changes. These local image patches of size 64 × 64 were sampled around interest points from images of three different scenes in different cities, namely, Liberty (New York), Notre Dame (Paris), and Half Dome (Yosemite). They are divided into matching pairs and nonmatching pairs. The correspondences of local patches were found by mapping between images using stereo depth maps obtained by the Photo Tourism [38] and the multiview stereo algorithm proposed by Michael Geosele et al. [18]. For each subset (scene), there are up to 500 K pairs of local image patches, with equal number of matching pairs and nonmatching pairs. The dataset can be downloaded from: http://www.cs.ubc.ca/~mbrown/patchdata/patchdata.html.

This dataset is widely used for evaluating methods of learning descriptors. The results are usually reported by the curve of "false positive rate versus true positive rate," and the false positive rate at 95 % recall (FPR@95 %). A true positive is a matching pair that is also classified as positive, i.e., the distance between their descriptors is below a threshold. Similarly, a false positive is a nonmatching pair that is classified as positive. By changing the distance threshold, one can obtain a number of operation points to form a curve of "false positive rate versus true positive rate." Based on the curve, it is easy to obtain the FPR@95 %.

6.1.2   Benchmarks for Object Recognition

6.1.2.1   Caltech 101 and Caltech 256

The Caltech object recognition dataset has two versions. In its first version which is known as Caltech-101 [16], it contains 101 categories and then was extended to 256 categories in Caltech-256 [19]. These images were obtained by searching keywords on the Internet and manually removing bad examples. There is a single prominent object appeared in each image with some background cluster. Mostly, the object is centered in the middle part of the image. Each image was labeled according to which category it belongs to. They can be downloaded from: http://www.vision.caltech.edu/Image_Datasets/Caltech101/ and http://www.vision.caltech.edu/Image_Datasets/Caltech256/.

These two datasets have been widely used for the evaluation of generic object recognition/image classification. The averaged recognition rate across all categories is reported for comparison.

6.1.2.2   PASCAL VOC

The PASCAL Visual Object Classes (VOC) [10, 11] is a publicly available dataset of images together with groundtruth annotation and standardized evaluation software. All images in the dataset were collected from Flickr with large variation in size, viewpoint, pose, illumination, scale, and background cluster. It is widely used as a benchmark for evaluation of generic object recognition. The latest version is PASCAL VOC 2012, when the challenge is finished and no longer organized. The PASCAL VOC 2012 contains a set of 11,540 images for 20 classes as the training/validation data. Each image has an annotation file giving the bounding box and the class label for each object in the image. Since there may be multiple objects presented in one image, these images contain 27,450 objects in total. The groundtruth of the test data is not available, but there is an evaluation server for new methods to get their performance on the test data. The performance of object recognition on this dataset is usually judged by the precision–recall curve. So the average precision (AP) is the principal quantitative measure for each class, and the mean average precision (mAP) is for the whole dataset. The dataset and the evaluation tools can be downloaded from: http://host.robots.ox.ac.uk/pascal/VOC/index.html.

The PASCAL VOC Challenge has been a long time as the standard dataset and evaluation for generic object recognition task (or image classification). There were annual events hold along with major vision conferences from 2006 to 2012, supplying the standardized evaluation procedure to evaluate the performance of each submitted result. These challenges were participated by top researchers all over the world in the area of object recognition to test their algorithms in a worldwide objective and comparable platform. Now its role has been replaced by a much larger dataset, ImageNet, which we will introduce in the next.

6.1.2.3 ImageNet

While researchers were pursuing more difficult and larger scale dataset both for developing robust and scalable new recognition algorithms and for a thorough evaluation of existing ones, the ImageNet was released in 2009 [8]. Now, ImageNet is the largest scale image database publicly available in the vision community. It contains more than 1 million annotated images as training data, covering 1,000 categories organized by the hierarchical structure of WordNet [17]. Each category has on average more than 1,000 clean and high-resolution images. In this way, ImageNet supplies a high-quality dataset both in quality and quantity. Except for the 2010s challenge, the groundtruth of test data is not released to ensure that no algorithm is tuned toward the test data. Similar to the PASCAL VOC, it supplies a standardized online evaluation. More information as well as the dataset can be found on: http://www.image-net.org/.

6.1.3 Benchmarks for Image Retrieval

6.1.3.1 Oxford Buildings Dataset

This dataset is collected by Philbin et al. [34] for evaluating performance of image retrieval systems. It contains 11 different landmarks in the Oxford, which were retrieved from Flickr by querying their names, such as "Oxford Christ Church," "Oxford Radcliffe Camera," and so on. The distractor images were collected by searching "Oxford." There are totally 5,062 images of size 1024×768 collected in this dataset. For this reason, it is also known as Oxford 5 K dataset in some literature. For each landmark, there are five different query images, each of which has a region indicating the object of interest.

The groundtruth for each query region was labeled manually by searching over the entire dataset. According to whether the query region is appeared in the image or not and how good does it appear, one of the four possible labels was generated: (1) Good—a nice, clear picture of the retrieved object; (2) OK—more than 25 % of the object is clearly visible; (3) Junk—less than 25 % of the object is visible, or there is a very high level of occlusion or distortion; and (4) Absent—the object is not present. The number of Good and OK images ranges from 7 to 220 for different queries.

The mean average precision (mAP) is used as the measure to evaluate the overall performance of an image retrieval system. The average precision (AP) is defined as the area under the curve of "precision versus recall" for a query, in which precision is computed as the ratio of correctly retrieved images to the total retrieved images, and recall is computed as the ratio of correctly retrieved images to the total images corresponding to the query in the dataset. By changing the number of retrieved images, one can obtain this curve for a query. mAP is computed by averaging APs over all queries. In computing mAP, the images with labels 'Good' and 'OK' are considered as correctly retrieved images, while the images with label 'Absent' are considered as incorrectly retrieved images. For the images with 'Junk,' they are treated as they are not in the database, i.e., they do not involved in computation of both precision and recall.

This dataset is available on: http://www.robots.ox.ac.uk/~vgg/data/oxbuildings/. Besides, there is also available an additional set of distractor images of size 1024 × 768, which were collected by crawling from Flickr's 145 most popular tags. There are 99,782 images in this additional dataset. Using this distractor dataset, one can further test the scalability of an image retrieval system.

Similar to Oxford 5 K, Philbin et al. [35] also collected a dataset from Paris, containing 6,300 images with 55 queries. It is considered to be an independent dataset from Oxford 5 K and is thus commonly used together with Oxford 5 K, training on one dataset and testing on another to evaluate the generalizability of learning algorithms. It is available on: http://www.robots.ox.ac.uk/~vgg/data/parisbuildings/.

6.1.3.2 Kentucky's Recognition Benchmark

The Recognition Benchmark dataset proposed by Kentucky University's researchers [31] contains 10,200 images from 2,550 daily objects. Each object has four images of size 640 × 480 taken from different viewpoints. It has been used for evaluating performance of both specific object recognition and image retrieval approaches. The dataset can be downloaded from: http://www.vis.uky.edu/~stewe/ukbench/.

The dataset is usually tested by setting each of its images as a query, and return the top four images from the dataset. The number of correctly returned images is recorded. This procedure is repeated for all images, and the average of these numbers is reported as the measure of how good a tested approach is. A perfect result is 4 which means that all the images are correctly recognized/retrieved, while the worst result is 1 that means only the identical images are correctly recognized/retrieved. An even worse result is 0, indicating even the identical images are not among the returned images. However, this rarely happens as almost all approaches can give a high similarity score to the identical image.

6.1.3.3 INRIA Holidays

The Holidays dataset [24] mainly contains images collected from personal holiday photos. The remaining ones were taken on purpose to test robustness to various transformations, such as viewpoint change, illumination change, image rotation, image blur, and so on. There are totally 1,491 images in this dataset, covering various scene types, ranging from natural ones to man-made ones. These images are divided into 500 groups, each of which is a distinct scene/object. In evaluation of image retrieval, the first image of each group is used as query, and so the remaining images in the group are groundtruth. Similar to the Oxford Building dataset, the Holidays dataset also supplies with a distractor set of 1 million images downloaded from Flickr. mAP is the most widely used evaluation measure for this dataset. The dataset as well as the precomputed SIFT descriptors can be downloaded from: http://lear.inrialpes.fr/~jegou/data.php.

6.2   Conclusion Remarks and Future Work

Since the beginning of the 1990s, the local image descriptors have been studied for more than two decades in the computer vision community. Many kinds of properties in a local image patch have been explored in order to get a robust and discriminative descriptor, such as moment invariants, responses on steerable filters, image gradient, intensity relationship, and so on. Among these properties, image gradient and intensity relationship are the two main streams in designing local image descriptor. Especially after the performance evaluation conducted by Mikolajczyk and Schmid [27], almost all the newly developed methods are based on them, for example, CS-LBP [23] is based on intensity relationship between center symmetric points; LIOP [41] is based on intensity relationship among four neighboring points; SMD [20] and many handcrafted binary descriptors (BRISK [26], BRIEF [6], FREAK [2], etc.) are based on intensity comparisons between some predefined locations; KAZE [3] is based on the gradient computed on a nonlinear scale space; and MROGH [14] is based on the gradient computed in a rotationally invariant way. Until very recently, machine learning techniques have been used in designing local image descriptors as an alternate to the traditional handcrafted descriptors, both for the traditional float-type descriptors [5, 37] and the burgeoning binary descriptors [13, 39]. Promising results are observed on some datasets. Although some learning-based descriptors have shown good generalized ability to other dataset, it still lacks a large scale and hence convincing evaluation. Even though we have to point out that for the difficult image matching problems, the learning-based descriptors could be a reasonable solution if one can obtain high-quality training data. On the basis of the previous published work, we have the following observations:

(1) Image gradient could be a first choice of low-level image property for designing a local image descriptor as it is robust in a wide range of image transformations and captures discriminative information. Moreover, it is easy to use. When using intensity, if it is designed carefully, higher performance can be achieved. One remark about using intensity for local image description is that it has to be encoded in a way at least invariant to monotonic changes, because this is one of the largest motivations for using it. Almost all the high-performance descriptors based on intensity in the literature have this characteristic.

(2) As the predominant methodology for designing local image descriptors is handcrafted, the labeled training samples do not play an essential role as those in object detection/image classification. The main purpose of providing standard image matching dataset is to evaluate different methods and give feedbacks to researchers for new ideas. For the similar reason, there are no large-scale labeled patch datasets until recently, when researchers began to study on utilizing machine learning for

designing local descriptors automatically. However, since the only available dataset of (non-)matching patches (introduced in Sect. 6.1.1.3) tends to be overfitted after several years' study, new challenging dataset is required for further improvements of learning-based descriptors, especially for developing high-performance descriptors with the help of deep neural networks, which has been a very successful learning paradigm for various vision tasks in recent years.

(3) Although binary descriptors still cannot beat the best float-type descriptors, the performance gap is not large. Since in most applications, feature matching is only the first step and the following steps can tolerate mismatches to some extent. Therefore, binary descriptors are as competent as float-type descriptors to many visual applications. In some applications (for instance, SLAM introduced in Sect. 5.4) which have a strict requirement on running time, binary descriptors are preferable. This is because that many binary descriptors outperform the most efficient float-type descriptor (SURF [4]). Meanwhile, using binary descriptors usually requires less memory to store descriptors than SURF. We have to note that although matching binary descriptors can be executed extremely fast in the modern computers by machine instructions, it is still too slow if we have to match millions of them, which often happens in image retrieval and large-scale structure from motion. In these cases, matching float-type descriptors with an approximate nearest neighbor search algorithm is remarkably faster than directly matching binary descriptors. Many researchers have noticed this problem and proposed several solutions [9, 32, 40] for fast nearest neighbor searching of binary descriptors, but it still has much work to do within this scope.

(4) For some difficult cases, there is still no descriptor that is capable of dealing with. These problems include matching images with repetitive patterns, large viewpoint changes, severe illumination changes (not the monotonic ones, but are complex ones usually caused by seasons, day and night switch, local lighting), and matching heterogeneous images (mostly, for images captured in remote sensing from various types of sensors, such as Synthetic Aperture Radar (SAR) images, infrared images, and optical images). There are already some initial solutions [7, 12, 15, 22, 29] for some of them, but they are far from practical applications. Much more work is definitely required.

Based on the above observations, in the authors' opinion, the following directions are worthy for us to devote efforts in the future.

- *Designing specific descriptors for extremely hard cases* In the past, local descriptors are proposed to be useful in as many cases as possible. Therefore, researchers tried hard to conquer all possible negative influences in their descriptors. Until now, local descriptors work well in cases of small to medium scale change and blur, in-plane rotation, noise, not very large viewpoint change, and linear or monotonic globally brightness change. Unfortunately, there is no free meal in the world. While it is possible to achieve a satisfactory trade off among various photometric and geometric transformations if they are not severe, it is hard in case of severe transformations. As a result, for those extremely hard cases described in the above paragraph, we should tackle them one by one, each with a kind of specific descriptor. Another reason for moving research effort to these hard challenges is that if we still focus on pursuing better descriptors to those already solved transformations (at least for most cases), it only helps a little for related applications as most of them are tolerable for a certain amount of mismatches. Among these difficult situations, dealing with very large viewpoint changes may need to be associated with a robust interest region detector. For the other cases, especially about severe illumination changes, it requires better feature description method.

- *Learning binary descriptors* Both learning image descriptors and designing binary descriptors are promising in this area. Therefore, it is reasonable to research on their intersected topic: learning binary descriptors. Furthermore, learning binary descriptors directly from the local image patch is more attractive than from an intermediate representation, because computing an intermediate representation not only requires more processing time, but also limits the performance of the learned descriptor. Currently, the learning paradigm for this purpose can be summarized as first designing a set of available binary features, then using feature selection to obtain the descriptor. Apparently, how to design computationally efficient and discriminative binary features is still a key problem and deserves more efforts. Moreover, it is worth to point out that innovation on this learning paradigm may lead to significant improvement. Inspired by the large success of deep learning in computer vision, it is expected that it will be applied to learn binary descriptor in the near future. In fact, there already emerges some pioneer work in utilizing deep neural networks to learn high-performance patch descriptors [21, 25, 33, 36, 42], but most of them are float-type vectors.
- *Fast indexing methods for binary descriptor* One of the most attractive properties of binary descriptors is that their Hamming distance can be fast computed. However, as pointed out in our observations, when we have to search for nearest neighbors in a very large scale, computing all the Hamming distances is time consuming and does not scale well. In this case, it requires a fast (approximate) nearest neighbor search method for binary descriptors. If this problem is not addressed satisfactorily, it will largely restrict the application of binary descriptors.
- *Various applications of binary descriptor* Currently, binary descriptor is not used as much as float-type descriptor in visual applications. Only a few tasks which are based on image matching are reported with binary descriptors, such as template matching for camera track used in augmented reality, SLAM, and specific object recognition in a small range. Apparently, binary descriptor requires more applications to demonstrate its power as well as encourage researchers to study more on this area.

References

1. Aanæs, H., Dahl, A., Steenstrup Pedersen, K.: Interesting interest points. Int. J. Comput. Vis. **97**, 18–35 (2012)
2. Alahi, A., Ortiz, R., Vandergheynst, P.: FREAK: Fast retina keypoint. In: IEEE Conference on Computer Vision and Pattern Recognition, pp. 510–517 (2012)

3. Alcantarilla, P., Bartoli, A., Davison, A.: KAZE features. In: European Conference on Computer Vision, pp. 214–227 (2012)
4. Bay, H., Ess, A., Tuytelaars, T., Gool, L.V.: SURF: speeded up robust features. Comput. Vis. Image Underst. **110**(3), 346–359 (2008)
5. Brown, M., Hua, G., Winder, S.: Discriminative learning of local image descriptors. IEEE Trans. Pattern Anal. Mach. Intell. **33**(1), 43–57 (2011)
6. Calonder, M., Lepetit, V., Ozuysal, M., Trzcinski, T., Strecha, C., Fua, P.: BRIEF: computing a local binary descriptor very fast. IEEE Trans. Pattern Anal. Mach. Intell. **33**(7), 1281–1298 (2012)
7. Dellinger, F., Delon, J., Gousseau, Y., Michel, J., Tupin, F.: SAR-SIFT: a SIFT-like algorithm for SAR images. IEEE Trans. Geosci. Remote Sens. **53**(1), 453–466 (2015)
8. Deng, J., Dong, W., Socher, R., Li, L.J., Li, K., Fei-Fei, L.: Imagenet: a large-scale hierarchical image database. In: IEEE Conference on Computer Vision and Pattern Recognition, pp. 248–255 (2009)
9. Esmaeili, M., Ward, R., Fatourechi, M.: A fast approximate nearest neighbor search algorithm in the hamming space. IEEE Trans. Pattern Anal. Mach. Intell. **34**(12), 2481–2488 (2012)
10. Everingham, M., Eslami, S.M.A., Van Gool, L., Williams, C.K.I., Winn, J., Zisserman, A.: The pascal visual object classes challenge: a retrospective. Int. J. Comput. Vis. **111**(1), 98–136 (2015)
11. Everingham, M., Van Gool, L., Williams, C.K.I., Winn, J., Zisserman, A.: The pascal visual object classes (VOC) challenge. Int. J. Comput. Vis. **88**(2), 303–338 (2010)
12. Fan, B., Huo, C., Pan, C., Kong, Q.: Registration of optical and SAR satellite images by exploring the spatial relationship of the improved SIFT. IEEE Geosci. Remote Sens. Lett. **10**(4), 657–661 (2013)
13. Fan, B., Kong, Q., Trzcinski, T., Wang, Z., Pan, C., Fua, P.: Receptive fields selection for binary feature description. IEEE Trans. Image Process. **23**(6), 2583–2595 (2014)
14. Fan, B., Wu, F., Hu, Z.: Aggregating gradient distributions into intensity orders: a novel local image descriptor. In: IEEE Conference on Computer Vision and Pattern Recognition, pp. 2377–2384 (2011)
15. Fan, B., Wu, F., Hu, Z.: Towards reliable matching of images containing repetitive patterns. Pattern Recogn. Lett. **32**(14–15), 1851–1859 (2011)
16. Fei-Fei, L., Fergus, R., Perona, P.: Learning generative visual models from few training examples: an incremental bayesian approach tested on 101 object categories. In: IEEE Conference on Computer Vision and Pattern Recognition Workshop on Generative-Model Based Vision (2004)
17. Fellbaum, C.: WordNet: An Electronic Lexical Database. Bradford Books (1998)
18. Goesele, M., Snavely, N., Curless, B., Hoppe, H., Seitz, S.: Multi-view stereo for community photo collections. In: International Conference on Computer Vision, pp. 1–8 (2007)
19. Griffin, G., Holub, A., Perona, P.: Caltech-256 object category dataset. In: Technical Report 7694, California Institute of Technology (2007)
20. Gupta, R., Mittal, A.: SMD: a locally stable monotonic change invariant feature descriptor. In: European Conference on Computer Vision, pp. 265–277 (2008)
21. Han, X., Leung, T., Jia, Y., Sukthankar, R., Berg, A.: MatchNet: unifying feature and metric learning for patch-based matching. In: IEEE Conference on Computer Vision and Pattern Recognition, pp. 3279–3286 (2015)
22. Hauagge, D., Snavely, N.: Image matching using local symmetry features. In: IEEE Conference on Computer Vision and Pattern Recognition, pp. 206–213 (2012)
23. Heikkila, M., Pietikainen, M., Schmid, C.: Description of interest regions with local binary patterns. Pattern Recognit. **42**, 425–436 (2009)
24. Jegou, H., Douze, M., Schmid, C.: Hamming embedding and weak geometric consistency for large scale image search. In: European Conference on Computer Vision, pp. 304–317 (2008)
25. Lai, H., Pan, Y., Liu, Y., Yan, S.: Simultaneous feature learning and hash coding with deep neural networks. In: IEEE Conference on Computer Vision and Pattern Recognition, pp. 3270–3278 (2015)

26. Leutenegger, S., Chli, M., Siegwart, R.: BRISK: binary robust invariant scalable keypoints. In: International Conference on Computer Vision, pp. 2548–2555 (2011)
27. Mikolajczyk, K., Schmid, C.: A performance evaluation of local descriptors. IEEE Trans. Pattern Anal. Mach. Intell. **27**(10), 1615–1630 (2005)
28. Mikolajczyk, K., Tuytelaars, T., Schmid, C., Zisserman, A., Matas, J., Schaffalitzky, F., Kadir, T., Gool, L.V.: A comparison of affine region detectors. Int. J. Comput. Vis. **65**(1–2), 43–72 (2005)
29. Mishkin, D., Matas, J., Perdoch, M.: MODS: fast and robust method for two-view matching. CoRR abs/1503.02619 (2015)
30. Moreels, P., Perona, P.: Evaluation of features detectors and descriptors based on 3d objects. Int. J. Comput. Vis. **73**(3), 263–284 (2007)
31. Nistér, D., Stewénius, H.: Scalable recognition with a vocabulary tree. In: IEEE Conference on Computer Vision and Pattern Recognition, pp. 2161–2168 (2006)
32. Norouzi, M., Punjani, A., Fleet, D.: Fast exact search in hamming space with multi-index hashing. IEEE Trans. Pattern Anal. Mach. Intell. **36**(6), 1107–1119 (2014)
33. Osendorfer, C., Bayer, J., Urban, S., van der Smagt, P.: Convolutional neural networks learn compact local image descriptors. In: International Conference on Neural Information Processing, pp. 624–630 (2013)
34. Philbin, J., Chum, O., Isard, M., Sivic, J., Zisserman, A.: Object retrieval with large vocabularies and fast spatial matching. In: IEEE Conference on Computer Vision and Pattern Recognition, pp. 1–8 (2007)
35. Philbin, J., Chum, O., Isard, M., Sivic, J., Zisserman, A.: Lost in quantization: improving particular object retrieval in large scale image databases. In: IEEE Conference on Computer Vision and Pattern Recognition, pp. 1–8 (2008)
36. Simo-Serra, E., Trulls, E., Ferraz, L., Kokkinos, I., Fua, P., Moreno-Noguer, F.: Discriminative learning of deep convolutional feature point descriptors. In: International Conference on Computer Vision (2015)
37. Simonyan, K., Vedaldi, A., Zisserman, A.: Learning local feature descriptors using convex optimisation. IEEE Trans. Pattern Anal. Mach. Intell. **36**(8), 1573–1585 (2014)
38. Snavely, N., Seitz, S.M., Szeliski, R.: Photo tourism: exploring photo collections in 3D. ACM Trans. Graph. **25**, 835–846 (2006)
39. Trzcinski, T., Christoudias, M., Lepetit, V.: Learning image descriptors with boosting. IEEE Trans. Pattern Anal. Mach. Intell. **37**(3), 597–610 (2015)
40. Trzcinski, T., Lepetit, V., Fua, P.: Thick boundaries in binary space and their influence on nearest-neighbor search. Pattern Recogn. Lett. **33**(16), 2173–2180 (2012)
41. Wang, Z., Fan, B., Wu, F.: Local intensity order pattern for feature description. In: International Conference on Computer Vision, pp. 603–610 (2011)
42. Zagoruyko, S., Komodakis, N.: Learning to compare image patches via convolutional neural networks. In: IEEE Conference on Computer Vision and Pattern Recognition, pp. 4353–4361 (2015)

Printed in the United States
By Bookmasters